Body Language for Competent Teachers

Nonverbal skills are invaluable for teachers in 'getting the message across' to classes and understanding the messages pupils are sending – messages of interest or messages of confrontation, which are first expressed non-verbally. With increasing interest in classroom competence, teachers need to understand the use of gesture, posture, facial expression and tone of voice. These have become especially important for effective teachers in a climate where respect has to be earned rather than coming automatically with the job.

Each chapter of the book has training exercises related to its theme for the new teacher; answers are provided at the end of each chapter. The last chapter is addressed to staff responsible for staff training and development, especially in the school context, and includes suggestions for half- and whole-day courses.

Sean Neill has been carrying out research on non-verbal communication at the University of Warwick over the last ten years, and has taught, and published numerous research papers and an academic book, *Classroom Nonverbal Communication*.

Chris Caswell is a member of the Senior Management Team at Myton School, Warwick and has wide-ranging teaching experience. He has taught school-based courses on classroom non-verbal skills at Myton and other schools, and related courses in other institutions, as well as counselling many inexperienced colleagues.

Body Language for Competent Teachers

Sean Neill and Chris Caswell

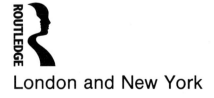

London and New York

First published 1993
by Routledge
11 New Fetter Lane, London EC4P 4EE

Simultaneously published in the USA and Canada
by Routledge
29 West 35th Street, New York, NY 10001

Typeset in 10/12pt Palatino by Witwell Ltd, Southport

Printed in Great Britain by
Clays Ltd, St Ives PLC

A catalogue reference for this title is available from the British Library
ISBN 0-415-06660-3

Library of Congress Cataloging in Publication Data
Neill, S. R. St. J. (Sean Rupert St. John), 1945-
    Body language for competent teachers / Sean Neill and Chris
Caswell.
        p.   cm.
    Includes bibliographical references (p.   ) and indexes.
    ISBN 0-415-06660-3
    1. Nonverbal communication in education—Great Britain—Problems,
exercises, etc. 2. Teachers—Training of—Great Britain—Problems.
exercises, etc. 3. Interaction analysis in education. I. Caswell,
Chris, 1950- . II. Title.
LB1033.5.N44   1992
371.1'22—dc20   92-24744
                                                                CIP

For our children
Clare, Richard, Riki, Rupert, Samantha and Suzannah
and their teachers
Celia and Liz

Contents

Acknowledgements   ix
General note   xi
Preface — who this book is for   xiii

1 Introduction   1
2 What is non-verbal communication?   9
3 Stage directions and props   25
4 Pupil behaviour and deviancy   42
5 The meaning of pupils' non-verbal signals   55
6 Getting attention   77
7 Conveying enthusiasm   99
8 Confrontations; or the Empire Strikes Back   128
9 Relationships with individual children   155
10 Implications for trainers   182

References   195
Further reading   198
Author index   201
Subject index   203

Acknowledgements

Much of the research on which this book is based was funded by the Nuffield Foundation. We are grateful to the colleagues who have assisted us, especially John Robertson, and to our families for their forbearance over many years. Our greatest debt is to the teachers and children from whom we have learnt so much, and especially to those who have participated in our research, at no direct benefit to themselves, but, we hope, to the benefit of those who follow them.

General note

We have generally referred to the teacher as 'you' in the text; for clarity we refer to individual children as 'he' and teachers as 'she', except when dealing with particular individuals or the small amount of behaviour specific to one sex. In the great majority of cases, teacher and pupil behaviour relates to their roles irrespective of sex.

As discussed in Chapter 2, there is little research evidence in the United Kingdom on ethnic differences in classroom non-verbal communication. Unshaded line drawings have been used for clarity, including in illustrations based on photographs or recordings of blacks. To preserve anonymity, sex and appearance have been changed, except where they are critical to the points made from an illustration.

Preface — who this book is for

This book is intended for new classroom teachers, including licensed and articled teachers, and those who advise and train them. The section on initial encounters with groups will be valuable to many others who have the same need as teachers to show authority, such as youth group workers and playground supervisors. Workers with adults and youth trainers, as well as teachers, have to arouse the interest of their listeners and communicate interest in them and their efforts. Many of the techniques are also valuable to those dealing with groups of adults – though hopefully they will not need our advice on dealing with disruption. We have addressed the main text to 'you' as the inexperienced practitioner.

Each section of the book includes exercises which readers can use on a self-instructional basis. At the end of the book we include guidance for people running courses for colleagues, especially on how they can phase the exercises and on collecting and using material for more advanced work in in-service and initial courses. Some techniques, such as videotaping course participants, are potentially challenging and distressing for those involved, especially those who are already having difficulties and who could potentially benefit most from such a course. As a course leader you must therefore tread carefully. Our advice on course arrangement is based on experience of what engages the interest and involvement of participants, without stressing them unduly. We can't guarantee that this will work in *your* situation, but it should!

Our ideas and conclusions are based on research evidence as well as practical experience. Much of the original research is published in academic journals which are only available in specialist libraries, but there are several books available (including Sean Neill's *Classroom Nonverbal Communication*) which give more detailed surveys of this research. If you want to follow up a particular point, the books listed under 'Further Reading' have full reference lists which will allow you to follow up topics in more detail.

Except in a few cases where a topic is only covered in journal articles (for example, the assessments of what kinds of training course on classroom non-verbal research work, covered in Chapter 10) we refer as far as possible to books which are fairly readily available.

TRAINING – AND SELF-TRAINING – MATERIALS

At the end of each chapter we include exercises and discussion topics. So why put exercises in this book? Well, they are there for three reasons. Firstly they should help you to clarify some of the issues that we raise during the chapters by applying them to a specific set of images or circumstances – a sort of 'test yourself' exercise! The value of active learning applies in this area too. Secondly, they will allow you to apply your existing knowledge (and there will be a lot of it!) to given situations, thereby accentuating the principle that teachers can and do use non-verbal strategies as part of their coping armoury. Thirdly, they should allow you to define and develop strategies on an accumulating basis, by applying what you have learned so far to easily understood and recognisable situations. Simply stated, the exercises should, collectively, help you to develop your knowledge and understanding of non-verbal communication and suggest how you can apply it to actual classroom situations.

In order to achieve this our exercises follow two distinct formats – pictorial and descriptive – each requiring a different response from you.

Firstly, there are 'Pictorial Exercises': 'What are these images saying?' Here we have used drawings to illustrate particular non-verbal signals or patterns of behaviour.

Each chapter will have a number of these exercises, requiring you to provide your own definitions as to what is probably happening, or what you think the image is saying. To help, we have provided our own definition or explanation for each exercise at the end of the chapter (working, of course, from the privileged position of knowing the situation from whence the images were taken!).

You should not be unduly concerned if your explanations vary slightly from ours, as images taken out of context can be ambiguous and misleading. Indeed, this is precisely the point we shall make repeatedly about how non-verbal signals are used: their ambiguity allows messages to be conveyed without either sender or receiver having to acknowledge them explicitly. This is most obvious when pupils want to be disruptive without overtly challenging you, or when you use ironic non-verbal signals to qualify an apparently innocuous verbal statement; but non-verbal signals can also have a more positive value. You can convey enthusiasm or praise non-verbally to pupils, who might reject it, if you gave it verbally, because of pressures from their peers.

The real value of these pictorial exercises lies in the process of attempting to define the meaning behind them and, by doing so, becoming more familiar with the potential of such signals. We hope to encourage you to watch your class in a more specific and structured way and to develop, over a period of time, a sort of 'thesaurus' or index of behaviours from which you will be able to predict more accurately the intention of the individuals within your class.

Secondly, there are 'Descriptive Exercises': 'What are these situations saying?' Here we are exploring non-verbal features in actual classroom situations (taken from our own experience) where even a series of drawn images would be unable to convey the full nature and complexity of the problem. We hope that the circumstances described in these exercises will be reasonably familiar to you, but if not, it is perfectly acceptable, indeed desirable, for you to modify the situations to fit individuals and circumstances known to and remembered by you from your teaching career, training or even from your own school-days!

Within these situations you are asked to consider what the non-verbal dimensions may be; what you can recognise and what is probably being conveyed. Again, we hope to encourage you to focus on those non-verbal behaviours that you already recognise and use, albeit often subconsciously, and to become more aware of those strategies and behaviours that form part of your pupils' repertoire.

These descriptive exercises may be particularly useful when used as part of group or pair situations, where you will be able to share ideas and may be more inclined to role-play or mimic particular stances or gestures. It takes courage to do this, but it is the quickest way of reminding yourself just how powerful non-verbal communication can be.

Where appropriate, many chapters will include comments on a number of common concerns associated with the chapter content. These will be set out in such a way as to outline the concern and suggest possible solutions. Of course there will be readers who will say, 'Well that won't work here!', or, 'What, with my class? They must be joking!' Clearly, any solution must suit the circumstances in which it is to apply (we explore this point more fully in the next section); we are acutely aware of the limitations of providing such 'words of wisdom'. However, finding a beginning may be half the solution and our thoughts may serve to trigger a reaction or discussion, which you and your colleagues can tailor to fit your own circumstances.

The exercises throughout the book are there to assist in your understanding of the concepts under discussion, but don't let them become intimidating. For many readers it may be sufficient simply to read through, and perhaps come back to the exercises later. Some may feel that the exercises (especially the 'Descriptive Exercises') are better suited to a whole-school INSET topic, where teachers have the opportunity to discuss the exercises, pooling their thoughts and experience. Whatever your response is, it should be remembered that no exercise, no matter how intricate or cleverly constructed, can replace the 'real life' experience that it is attempting to replicate. Your experiences are as valid as any, and your knowledge of non-verbal communication probably far more advanced than you have realised. If we can help you to focus your knowledge in such a way as to allow you to maintain an effective working relationship with and between the pupils in your charge, and still come away with some loose change in the sanity purse, we shall be pleased.

WILL IT WORK?

The training materials raise the question, 'Will it work?' To this the answer must be 'Usually'. Perhaps a little more detail, and a more theoretical approach to what we mean by 'usually', will help.

Forecasting what will work in a classroom situation has much in common with forecasting the weather. Despite the fact that weather is controlled by well-known physical processes, it is virtually impossible to predict exactly what it will be doing more than a few days ahead. This is because it is impossible to detect all the influences which are at work on a particular weather system, and the influence of the factors which are missed builds up rapidly. As a result, two situations which may appear to be identical can develop in different directions. However, weather is not completely unpredictable; some types of weather system are more stable and predictable than others, and we can make overall predictions even if we cannot predict in fine detail. Thus we cannot predict whether it will rain or not on Midsummer Day two years hence, but we can be sure it will not freeze. (Technically, weather can be described by chaos theory (the mathematical variety) – chaos theory, in all its forms, is only too familiar to most teachers.)

In the same way, we cannot be sure that a given behavioural tactic will *invariably* be successful in the classroom; you may have missed what another member of the class was doing previously; there may be school or home circumstances which influence pupils' reactions; you may in fact not be sending out the signals you think you are sending. However, it is most unlikely, for instance, that a flat, monotonous delivery will arouse the interest of an unenthusiastic class, or that a diffident approach will discipline them. The very fact that the signals we are dealing with have developed for purposes of communication means that most children will react to them in similar ways on the basis of their previous experience. In the same way, verbal commands will usually, but not always, have the expected effect. If you say 'Sit down' the class may not; however, they are more likely to than if you had said, 'Leave the room'.

Furthermore, non-verbal signals are more powerful in conveying feelings than speech because most recipients are less aware of them. If you overtly tell a class that the subject you are dealing with is really exciting, or that you intend to deal firmly with any indiscipline, the explicit message may give the more cynical members of the class a clear target to aim at. If you convey enthusiasm or firmness non-verbally, your audience extracts the message from your behaviour subliminally. Since they have derived the message themselves without being aware of having done so, they are less likely to be able to challenge it.

SUMMARY

The main text of the book is addressed to inexperienced teachers, with teacher trainers, especially at a school level, and other professionals who have similar communication problems as secondary audiences. The final chapter is primarily addressed to trainers. Though the book is research-based, its aim is practical training.

At the end of each chapter we will include exercises of two types. The first are for practitioners reading the book on their own; they are short exercises to test existing knowledge and what has been learnt from the chapter. The second set include descriptions of activity sequences which can be done independently or as a group and used as points for discussion. Most of these problems derive from crises which inexperienced teachers have reported to us; we suggest what might have gone wrong and possible ways in which the crisis could have been averted. We cannot guarantee that these suggestions will 'work' in a particular situation, but they have a high probability of doing so.

Chapter 1

Introduction

UP THE SWANEE?

The phrase 'The Blackboard Jungle' epitomises the frustrations, anxieties and cynicism of those involved in the stressful occupation of teaching. It aptly highlights the endless tangle of theoretical advice and pedagogical practice, populated with such strange creatures as reports, examinations, preparation, capitation, attainment targets, folklore and headteachers. Little wonder, then, that many student and probationary teachers enter the jungle well-schooled in identifying the fauna and flora, but wondering why their training has not armed them with a practical 'machete' with which to cut a preliminary path.

One particularly painful and thorny tangle for many new teachers is classroom control. Deviant and disruptive behaviour can divert them away from their carefully planned teaching programme, maybe never to return. It is easy for any experienced teacher to recall their early days in the classroom when survival ranked high on the list of priorities, and when endless evenings were spent worrying neurotically about certain classes and pupils.

Solutions were hard to come by; every promising path ended abruptly in a seething morass, and the class showed a mulish tendency to bolt in every direction but the right one. As a new teacher, you are in a position of having to break in a creature which you cannot directly force to do your bidding and which can collectively outrun you, both literally and metaphorically. We therefore make no apology for concentrating, at the outset, on how you can detect, from the laid-back ears or rolling eye, the signs of trouble which need your immediate attention, as well as where a more soothing approach is required. Secondly, we look at the 'hands'; the skills which allow you to establish and maintain effective control and authority – unless you meet a bucking bronco of a class. A very small number of children and classes are uncontrollable, even by the sanctions available to an experienced teacher.

However, you need to go further, not only to catch and tether, but to persuade the mule to follow, to set up an environment in which authority and control become merely subsidiary. Though we have left the positive side of the classroom relationship to last, this is not a reflection of its relative unimportance – any more than our omission of anything related to the curriculum means it does not matter what teachers teach. Children have instrumental views of their teachers (e.g. Docking 1980, Nash 1974) – they expect them to teach rather than to be friendly, and this expectation is likely to be increased with the National Curriculum.

Some may regret this lack of true friendship between teacher and class, but this phenomenon is not confined to the school. Among adults, friends are usually similar in age and status and friendships do not normally develop between work colleagues who occupy markedly different positions in the hierarchy. You cannot be truly a friend to the children, simply because you are an adult, and therefore you cannot establish a relationship based on true reciprocity. Inevitably you define the relationship, if only because if you fail to fulfil the children's expectations, they may consider themselves released from the need to attend (Nash 1974). Nash found that if the teacher did not meet the children's expectations that she should control and teach them, they rebelled against her; these were norms from which she was not readily allowed to depart. 'Friendliness is something of a bonus' as Nash says, and he feels that novice teachers need to learn the rules the class expects.

Perhaps the biggest hurdle to clear in arriving at an appropriate relationship lies in the very nature of most teachers. As a breed we tend to be sympathetic to the potential dangers and problems which can affect our charges, and we are usually intent upon establishing, as quickly as possible, an empathy from which we can cater for their individual needs. It is not surprising, therefore, that for so many years, teacher training courses should have concentrated on pupil-based methods. Courses in the sociology, psychology and philosophy of education have tended, most laudably, to place emphasis on the factors affecting pupil performance. Government departments and other bodies have made part of the basic student teacher vocabulary such expressions as 'equality of opportunity', 'special needs', 'moral danger' and 'core curricula'. No one is denying the immense importance of these factors or disputing their place within the training process, but you will not find yourself in a position where you have the power to influence school practice in response to these pastoral and curriculum needs for some period into your career. You are unlikely to get such influence until you have demonstrated effective classroom skills.

ALL THE CLASS A STAGE

Whole-class teaching is very different to most situations in the normal social environment for which everybody has extensively practised social skills. You need to accentuate some of your existing skills to deal with this situation, and to abandon others. In normal conversation, for example, most of us are skilled at detecting, from the relevant non-verbal signs, if we are boring our friends, and can shift the topic of conversation until we detect more interest; but you cannot allow the children the same freedom to dictate the curriculum.

In the last resort, teachers have no sanction which can cow a child into submission (given that he has not been suspended from the school!) and in an average-sized class you cannot physically stop a number of children who are determined to be disruptive. Ultimately you cannot force children to learn; you must persuade them that to attend to what you propose to teach them is preferable to any alternative activity. Your chances of doing so are much greater if you can present your material in an interesting way and when the class cooperate with you, reward them in a way which they appreciate.

Many readers may wonder why it is necessary to look at non-verbal behaviour in such detail. Does it really matter whether you stand with your hands on your hips, or lean back against your desk? As we hope to show, it does. Readers may also wonder whether these aspects of performance are what teaching is all about. We would not wish to claim that they are, but research suggests that student teachers who were able to see their lessons as a performance which might be more or less successful managed better than those who were more completely and personally involved. Those who maintained a degree of detachment were more able to perform successfully. Self-knowledge, including awareness of one's non-verbal skills, leads to effective performance.

The success or failure of any lesson will hinge on the effective use of the communication skills at your disposal. These should form part of your authority, felt subjectively by your class as linking you to the structure of your school. It may seem odd that such skills are observed by pupils and are understood in the sense that they convey authority. Political speeches offer a parallel – some politicians are more effective speakers than others; a few are really charismatic. The ability to speak persuasively can make a major contribution to political success, but Atkinson (1984) has shown that it depends on remarkably simple techniques. Effective speakers tend to package their ideas in formats, such as contrasts and three-part lists ('Never in the field of human conflict has so much been owed by so many to so few') which make it easy for an audience to predict when the speaker will finish making a point; they can then respond immediately. Speaker and audience then seem to be 'on the same wavelength' as each other. The natural assumption must then be that the speaker is particularly persuasive. In other words, the manner of delivery governs the response; because it is readily taken in, the audience will form their impression from the delivery, even if they remember little of the content.

Significantly, many of the signals used by politicians to coordinate an audience's response are conveyed not in the words spoken, but through the non-verbal 'back-up' given in the speaker's postural and facial cues, tone of voice and speech timing. Atkinson suggests that politicians have to use relatively simple techniques as this is the only way that the response of a large audience can be synchronised. Even so, speeches frequently misfire through faulty technique – if the audience cannot predict when to applaud, they either do not applaud at all, or only hesitantly, after an embarrassing silence. The speaker does not seem to be 'getting through'. Charismatic speakers often seem to be able to time their speech so that it overlaps with the audience's applause, but without the important points being drowned out; thus they appear to have to struggle to keep their audience's enthusiasm under control. Atkinson suggests that most interactions, involving smaller numbers, will be more complex, and this certainly seems to apply to teaching.

Formal or informal? And what about the subject?

The more informal the approach and the greater the part of the children in the smooth running of the lesson, the more subtle your classroom skills need to be to maintain their interest in tasks which some at least would not have chosen freely. In a generally formal school setting, as an inexperienced teacher you can derive considerable support from the structure of the school rules, provided that you make sure you know them thoroughly, and can conduct lessons which are effective even if your relationship with the class is rather cool and distant. In such a setting the pupils are equally aware of how, as teacher, you should show your authority; any shortfall on your behalf may be immediately perceived as a sign of weakness. 'Master teachers' in such schools, who are often highly popular with their classes, have much warmer and more humorous relationships with their pupils. You can aspire to this desirable situation only as your skills improve; as we shall show, such relationships depend on the class's knowledge of the limits you will allow. Experienced teachers who move to a new school are sometimes surprised by the sudden need to put effort into controlling their classes; they are not always aware how much they previously relied on their thorough, but subliminal, knowledge of the formal and informal procedures of their old school, and their reputation among the children.

More progressive and informal school settings make the inexperienced teacher's task easier in some ways, because there is less of a 'them and us' atmosphere to set the children against you. You still need authority to convince them that your subject is worth attending to, and to get them to work steadily through the difficult or dull areas which are present in every subject. Where children expect warm and non-restrictive relationships with teachers, you must exercise your authority on a narrow borderline between coldness and over-familiarity. Every school contains difficult children; in dealing with these in the more informal situation you may have to rely more on your own authority, whereas in the more traditional establishment a framework of rules would provide more assistance. In fact our videotapes show that the real differences between classroom processes in progressive and traditional schools are less great than the apparent ones, simply because the children at schools tend to have more similar attitudes than their teachers. In a progressive school children may have no uniform, address the teachers by their first names and come in freely to choose their own seats in the classroom, but this does not mean they will treat you as a friend; in a formal school, uniform, lining up outside the classroom before going to designated seats, and

Figure 1.1 Six pupils occupying their positions during Ms. Discord's lesson. The seating arrangement was of their choosing and held its own significance

addressing you as 'Sir' or 'Miss' are no guarantee of order – yet nor do they prevent warm relationships.

Just as the similarities between different schools arise because their children react to teachers in similar ways, so similar tactics apply across subject boundaries in the secondary school. When children move from History to Home Economics, they are still the same children, and the different subject matter does not mean a complete difference in the social relationship they have with their teachers. Children are generally unaware of the intellectual structure of the particular subject, as you understand it – this would require knowledge which they are still in the process of learning. You cannot rely on the appeal of your subject itself, or the lure of completing their understanding of a particular branch of knowledge, to appeal to any substantial number of your pupils. Some children, especially in the younger age-groups, will be keen to learn, whatever you do. The majority will learn if you make it emotionally rewarding – especially if the alternatives are unrewarding. Their learning depends on a satisfactory teacher/pupil relationship, which is likely to remain independent of and unconnected to specific subject structures.

Teachers usually see themselves as teachers of a particular subject, and often feel that it is only possible to learn useful lessons from other teachers of their own subject. Pupils are far more likely to be impressed by what is happening in your relationship with them than by the finer points of the subject. What is more, their like or dislike of you may powerfully affect their attitude to the subject, and indeed whether they continue or drop it when option choices become available.

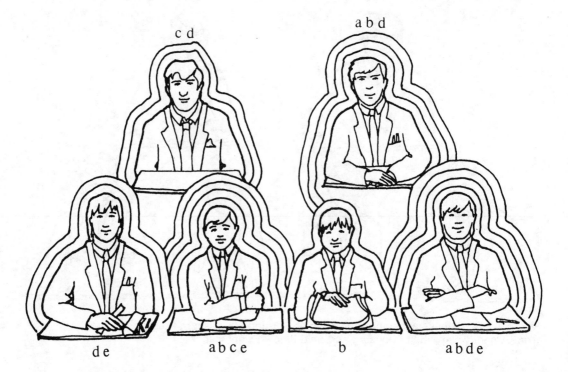

Figure 1.2 Shows the 'mitigators' affecting the pupils, each generally regarded as having potential for slowing or damaging pupils' educational progress:

a known family background conflicts
b reading age below 9:00
c probation, and or problems with the police
d anti-school/authority problems
e confirmed educational handicap other than low reading age (dyslexia etc.)

Hidden problems in the class

It is very likely that some of your pupils' performance will be affected by psychological or social factors which interfere with their learning. Recognising these factors, formal or informal, in or out of the classroom, is a skilled process, normally resulting from the gradual accumulation of evidence about the child concerned. As a new teacher you may be able to make some early identifications, but usually you will simply not have sufficient information at the start to make effective judgements or to devise independently an appropriate strategy to solve such problems. The words 'at the start' are crucial; if you wait until you have got to know the children so that you can react to them as individuals, the class will long since have made up its mind about you and will be acting accordingly. You have to get to know twenty-five or thirty children; they only have to get to know one teacher.

As we shall describe later, an experienced teacher often makes it quietly clear that

Figure 1.3 Shows the results of a like/dislike sociogram drawn from the results of questionnaires completed for the whole form. Only those responses relevant to this particular group are shown

Like for - - - - - - - / - - - - - - -
Dislike for ——————/————

she is in charge within half a minute of entering the room. Videotapes of a class as they encounter a new teacher sometimes show their dawning realisation that she is a 'soft touch' after only five or ten minutes. Let us take an actual example. Ms Discord, a probationer teacher of music in a large comprehensive school, found herself taking a particularly difficult class of third-year pupils. It was evident from her initial contacts with them that although immensely enthusiastic, well prepared and sympathetic, she was unable to make these factors count in terms of her relationship with the form. After only a few lessons, the 'honeymoon' period, she had serious discipline problems and the pupils lost interest in the subject as their challenges to her authority increased. It is not hard to imagine the frustration and anxiety which this situation produced – after all, her intentions were admirable. She had been told that the class were failing educationally, and that they had been labelled as failures. Armed with this limited information she had structured her lessons to cater for what she considered to be their probable individual needs. So what went wrong?

Firstly what she could not have known at the outset was the number and complexity of the problems affecting each pupil. Looking at these factors for just six members of that class, Figure 1.1 shows six boys as they sat during her lesson; Figure 1.2 shows how each of the six was affected by five well-known circumstances likely to interfere with their classroom performance. Already we have a complex pattern, likely to tax the skills of even the most experienced teacher.

Figure 1.3 adds a third factor. It is a like/dislike sociogram (a diagram of cliques, friendships and antipathies within a group) which, as well as looking like a schematic presentation of Custer's Last Stand, indicates the potential social flashpoints. A teacher who already knew the group might try to control seating positions so that potential opponents were out of reach, or at least keep a careful eye, for instance, that the boy in the front row was not being teased. As a new teacher you could run into further problems if your efforts to encourage this child antagonised the others, and you did not understand the reason for their recalcitrance.

Obviously, knowledge of the children's backgrounds and relationships can be helpful, but you cannot rely on having it, and must be able to cope without. Even if the information had been available to Ms Discord, she might have found it difficult to remember on the spur of the moment what related to whom. Many experienced teachers, in fact, purposely avoid getting the 'low-down' on a new class from its previous teacher, so that they start with a clean slate. They know that if a child has had a personality clash with the previous teacher, this will not necessarily recur with their different approach, provided they are not warned into going looking for trouble. *This makes it essential to be able to spot what is happening as it happens.* In the more formal classroom, this has to be done by watching the pupils.

What is clearly evident from this example is that in order to be effective, a teacher's sensitivity to the learning needs of pupils must go hand in hand with a structured and controlled working environment. Many of the pupils in this example did not see Ms Discord as holding any authority over them. Their rejection of her authority led to her punishing the class as a whole and hence to eventual resentment of the help she was offering. As Robertson (1989) suggests, pupils are well able to recognise what constitutes authority in their eyes, whether it is subject-based or based on skill in social dynamics. What Ms Discord lacked were those social skills which reflected the teacher's status and authority so she could hold the attention and direct the actions of the class. This was far more important than any specific or individual needs the boys had.

SUMMARY

The classroom situation and the teacher's role in it differ from normal social situations. This can cause problems for you as a new teacher, especially as the class may feel justified in disregarding teachers who do not conform to the teacher role as they expect it. Despite superficial differences, teacher–pupil relationships show many underlying similarities in formal and informal schools and the same interactional skills apply. These skills are valuable to you as a new teacher in dealing with class situations, because you are unlikely to have detailed knowledge of pupils' circumstances and backgrounds.

Chapter 2

What is non-verbal communication?

In this chapter we look at the types of signal covered by the term 'non-verbal communication'; the following chapters cover how they can be applied in particular circumstances. Non-verbal communication can be defined in a range of ways, but in this book we are concerned with non-verbal signals used in face-to-face interaction – mainly actual behaviour, but also signals such as dress and room arrangement which you or the children may 'set up' before you meet each other. These 'set up' signals allow you, more or less consciously, to plan ahead and alter what happens when you actually meet. We are excluding aspects such as the design and paint-scheme of your classroom, which are included as non-verbal communication by some authors, but over which you usually will have little influence.

In contrast to the approach in the rest of the book, where we look at the group of signals which are used in a particular context, such as getting attention, we will look here at each type of non-verbal signal in turn. We then need to look at the ways in which different individuals' use of non-verbal signals can vary. When we make rather definite statements below, on the uses of particular signals, this is based on English culture. Some types of non-verbal signal show more differences between cultures than others, and this is discussed in the last section of the chapter.

TYPES OF NON-VERBAL SIGNAL AND THEIR MEANINGS

We are mainly concerned with visual signals: facial expression, gaze, head and body posture, hand movements, interpersonal distance and spacing; other non-verbal signals such as the intonation and pace of speech, and dress, are covered more briefly.

Posture and spacing set the scene for an interaction between people. Under classroom conditions, use of space, personal distance, touch and posture are related. The message they convey depends on what else is happening at the time; they often indicate the intensity with which the main signal is being sent.

Gaze indicates attention and involvement. In most cases people do not look at each other continuously; the appropriate level of gaze varies between situations.

Facial expression plays a major role in conveying feelings. It can also be used to indicate to listeners what they should feel about the subject being discussed.

Intonation, like facial expression, can be used to show listeners how they should respond to what is being said. It can convey enthusiasm, authority and so on, but it also plays a major role in stressing the main and subsidiary elements of an explanation or argument. Timing in speech sends similar messages. Timing between speakers, especially the time a speaker or questioner is prepared to wait for a response (wait time), indicates aspects of the relationship such as the degree of respect for the other's contribution.

Hand movements fall into three main groups: wielding movements such as picking up and moving things, which do not have a communicative purpose; speech-related gestures which convey messages about the subject that is being talked about; and relationship-oriented signals. Under classroom conditions many of the latter are signals of dominance or control.

Posture and use of space

We deal with these signals first, because the layout and use of space in the classroom are usually set up by the teacher before teaching starts. They therefore help set the scene for the ensuing classroom drama. We can understand this most easily if we look first at personal distance and touch, to which spacing and layout are related.

Personal distance influences the intensity of a relationship or of a communication within a relationship. (Hence we speak metaphorically of being 'close' to someone, or of their being 'distant'.) If you approach pupils more closely, they will be more warmed by your praise, or more hurt by your criticism. A mild rebuke from close to is as threatening as a bellow from across the room; the increased intensity from proximity balances the reduced intensity of the signal itself. Reduced distance itself is ambiguous and conveys little information on its own, but it increases the anxiety the other person feels concerning what you intend.

If we reduce personal distance as far as possible, we touch. Though its meanings are the same as proximity, touch is an especially powerful and potentially threatening signal. The recipient of your other non-verbal and verbal signals can chose to disregard them, but if you can touch somebody you can physically force them to do what you want. Strict conventions therefore surround touch. As children grow older, and therefore less willing to accept praise, comfort or criticism from adults, their teachers have to be increasingly cautious in using touch. Right through education, though, pupils see some uses of touch as friendly and pleasurable, so the advice sometimes given that teachers should never touch children under any circumstances is excessive.

The significance of a reduction of individual distance, mentioned above, is largely due to the increased risk of touch which it implies.

Posture often indicates what a person's intentions are, in relation to personal distance. Leaning towards another person, whether sitting or standing, is an 'intention movement'; your intention, if you actually moved, would be to get closer to them. The posture therefore indicates increased intensity of communication, as does touch itself. Leaning away sends the opposite signal. Leaning over someone, or being higher than them, is dominant and potentially threatening because if you actually wanted to attack someone you could launch your attack better from above. Sitting or kneeling down to someone, at or below their level, is correspondingly non-threatening. Standing up is dominant, not only because it gives you height, but because it gives you freedom to move around and regulate your distance from pupils. Sitting down sends the opposite messages, especially if you then allow the pupils freedom to move around in their turn.

Classroom layout is a frozen formalisation of personal space. How the space is arranged, how individual pupils are positioned and who has freedom of movement are aspects of classroom organisation which send messages about how you intend to run the classroom. Very often the teacher's table is set apart, indicating a psychological distance between her and the children. In the formal classroom, children who sit at the front or in central positions are more involved than those on the periphery, distant from the teacher. Friends usually sit together if they are allowed to do so, and in the informal classroom, where they face each other, gaze adds to this closeness.

Gaze

There are some similarities between the amount of gaze and personal spacing. A child being reprimanded may often look down or away, avoiding your eye, to distance himself from the unpleasant experience.

Most classroom communication requires teacher and child to meet each other's eye, at least intermittently. Sustained gaze indicates close interest in the other person; like a close approach it can be stressful because you need further cues to interpret whether the attention is friendly or hostile. For this reason you may find the concentrated attention of a class disconcerting, especially if they use the concentration frown, described below.

Facial expression and head position

Both these sets of signals involve the head; but they are distinct and can be combined in various ways. Expression is the more important.

The effects of head position are often the same as those of posture on a smaller scale – a raised chin ('looking down your nose'), like standing over someone, is dominant; a bowed head, like kneeling down, is non-threatening. A distinctive signal, much used by some teachers, is the 'head cock', with the head over to one side, which signifies sympathetic interest.

Research shows that children, from the junior years on, judge whether the overall meaning of a non-verbal signal is friendly or negative primarily from the facial expression. Other aspects, such as gesture and posture, have a subsidiary influence.

Smiling and frowning are the most salient classroom expressions: the frown can cause confusion because it can imply concentration as well as threat or anger. The concentration frown looks exactly like a slight anger frown; the two cannot be told apart without other cues. They look the same apparently because a slight frown helps you see more clearly, whether what you are looking at interests or annoys you. Pupils may use the concentration frown when listening intently to you, or you may use it yourself, to stress what you are talking about, like the puzzled and surprised expressions described in the next paragraph.

These two common expressions – the puzzled brow and the surprised frown – are often used like gestures, to indicate how the pupils should respond to what you are saying. By using the appropriate brow expression you signal whether what you are talking about requires pupils' close attention, is difficult to understand, or is interesting and unexpected.

Intonation

Presenting examples of intonation really requires the use of a tape to accompany the book (as used by Brazil, Coulthard and Johns (1980)); the limited amount we can convey in writing does not mean that intonation is unimportant, however. The most important distinction is between 'proclaiming tone', which falls towards the end to the phrase, used for new information, and 'referring tone', which falls then rises towards the end, used for what is already known by the listener. In an explanation or a story, proclaiming tone marks the sections which advance the argument, referring tone those which fill in the detail. Children are sensitive to these differences in tone from an early age; pre-schoolers can use them appropriately when retelling a story.

Effective teachers have animated intonation; 'flat', unenthusiastic speech shows uncertainty. You can manipulate how you use the tones; if you use proclaiming tone repeatedly with the same information, by repeatedly indicating it is new and exciting you may improve the chance of the class actually taking it in. Equally, politicians, for example, use referring tone when talking about something controversial, to imply that all reasonable people accept their view. Other intonation patterns include the measured speech of authority and the hard tone of sarcasm, as well as the meaningful silence.

Gestures and hand signals

We have grouped speech-related gestures and relationship- or emotion-related hand movements together, though the messages they convey are very different.

Speech-related gestures serve two purposes. Firstly they can provide a concordance to the speech, marking out its structure and how it is to be interpreted. Secondly, if they carry some of the message, they force listeners to watch the speaker as well; if they only listen, they will miss part of the meaning. If it is not overdone, this can be an effective way of manipulating pupils' attention.

Animated speakers use gestures extensively to punctuate their speech (*beats*) and to illuminate the ideas they are talking about. Some subjects lend themselves to *pantomiming* (a biology teacher as a gorilla is a vivid memory from thirty years ago). More soberly, talk about shapes (such as the line of the trenches in the First World War, or the shape of a mathematical equation) or movements (such as rocks rolling along and eroding the bottom of a stream) may be illustrated by *iconic* gestures; the gesturing hand traces out the shape or imitates the movement. Mathematical ideas (or ideas in other subjects) can be represented by gestures as well as mathematical equations; as ideas have no physical form, these are *metaphoric* gestures. Mathematics is a precise subject, and this precision is represented by the forefinger-to-thumb precision grip being made in a vacuum. Thumb and finger carefully hold the invisible idea for the class's inspection. This is only one of a range of gestures which manipulate ideas as objects, to show the audience how they should be handled mentally.

There are various other hand movements which can be described as more relation-ship-oriented. Some, such as nominating whom is to talk next by pointing at them, or holding up a hand to stop them talking, are quick movements related to gesturing; but there is a range of more static hand postures, related to status and confidence. Folded arms, or hands on hips are dominating or threatening, while a range of fumbling or preening movements indicate stress or anxiety. You are most likely to use these at stressful points during the session, for instance during transitions from one class activity to another, when delay and disorganisation are possible.

GROUP DIFFERENCES IN SIGNALS

So far we have assumed that everyone receives the same message from the same non-verbal signals. However some non-verbal signals vary markedly in the way different people use them and the messages they convey, while others are much more stable.

What counts as fashionable dress, for example, changes, usually, from month to month. We may recognise a fashionably dressed teacher (or, within the limits of school uniform, a fashionably dressed child!) as being a particular kind of person, even though we are constantly having to look for something new.

On the other hand, a smile usually means pleasure (though if it is a sardonic smile, we may not share the pleasure), whether we see it in the classroom jungle or among the head-hunters of New Guinea. Film actually exists of first encounters between Westerners and isolated tribes in New Guinea, who were able to communicate quite effectively with each other despite no shared language. They shared signals for friendly and surprised expressions, though other non-verbal signals, such as those for counting, were different. Though we need to bear in mind individual and cultural differences in understanding non-verbal signals, if you could communicate reliably in Papua New Guinea, you *should* be able to get through to the natives of Papplewick.

In discussing the various types of non-verbal signal, we therefore distinguish between *universal* (e.g. smiling) and *culturally variable* signals (e.g. counting). Though this distinction is a bit over-simplified, it is useful in pointing out the types of signal – the culturally influenced ones – where possibilities for misunderstanding are greatest.

There is good evidence that the smile, for example, is a universal signal, based on genetic predispositions. We can be fairly confident of the meaning of such universal signals, though during childhood their use is affected by culture and individual experience. For example, the confident 'plus face' (looking down your nose at somebody) starts off in pre-school children as a universal and very definite signal, used in confrontations by the winner. With age it comes under more control by the child, and becomes more subtle. Dominant children use it in a wider range of situations, often when coping with non-social problems. In other words, older children tend to radiate 'effortless superiority'; their self-confidence is visible to others even before they interact with them. This self-confidence carries through to adulthood; student teachers who were confident at the time of their selection interview tended to do better on the course and when they got jobs.

Most facial expressions, gaze, body posture, interpersonal distance and hand movements such as pointing, fall into this group, in which the meaning of the signal is stable, but the accepted usage for it varies according to culture, or even within cultures. Though some facial expressions, such as that of fear, are universal, in some cultures (such as Japan) it may be bad form to show them in public. Equally, closeness and touch show affection and friendliness, but are bad form among men and older boys (except for footballers!) in England and America, but may freely be used by Arab, Eastern European or Italian men. As a result the Japanese may be seen as inscrutable and the English as cold and reserved by members of other cultures.

Culturally variable signals offer rich possibilities for misunderstanding. Two well-known gestures in the United Kingdom, the V-sign and the thumbs-up, are culturally based and learnt by each individual who uses them. However, if you go hitch-hiking in Sardinia you should beware of hailing a car with the thumbs-up, which is an obscene insult there. The driver thus accosted will express himself in no uncertain terms; however, he will be quite unimpressed by your V-sign in return, which in Sicily is an innocuous 'victory' or 'two'. Gestures and intonation are the most prominent groups of culturally variable signals.

When a signal is culturally variable, we must look out for misunderstanding between members of different cultural groups. If you are teaching ethnic minority children you should be on your guard against misunderstanding such signals, and being misunderstood when you use them yourself. When a signal is universal, problems may arise not with the signal itself, but because its use reflects different understandings of the situation. Thus a downcast gaze means subservience, but Western teachers often want children who are being reprimanded to look at them. This can lead to problems if the child being reprimanded comes from a culture which stresses obedience to elders (American teachers have had problems of this sort with American Indian children) or shares the teacher's culture, but is withdrawn or shy, and therefore finds looking at the teacher, with its undertone of challenge, too risky and stressful. On the other hand, among American black children, for instance, returning the teacher's gaze is defiant.

The teacher unwittingly helps them to subvert her authority by requiring them to look at her.

Unfortunately there is little research on cultural differences in non-verbal communication among schoolchildren in Britain. Most of the available research is on American children, especially black children. This indicates, for example, that black children tend to stand closer to each other and to touch more than white children. English pre-school teachers tend to touch black children, especially boys, more. This has been interpreted as control, with the teachers being stricter with black boys; but English black children may interpret the touch as friendly, in line with their American counterparts. We do not know if American and English black children behave similarly, and we have hardly any information on other important groups, such as Asian children. American research suggests that the non-verbal behaviour of adults from immigrant groups changes over generations as they settle in, but there is no corresponding information for children in England. Children learn to speak English with the local dialect, but we do not know if their non-verbal communication takes on the corresponding 'dialect'.

This last point is one reason to be cautious in assuming children will necessarily have communication difficulties. If they continue to have problems, this would reflect prejudice rather than poor communications. A further point from American research is that parents often see education as a critical route by which their children can advance in a potentially hostile environment. They may therefore resent teachers who seem to them to be making undue allowances for their children out of a misplaced sense of equality, thereby permitting them to cut themselves off from vital opportunities. This means you must try to find out what not only children but also their parents perceive and understand in educational situations.

INDIVIDUAL DIFFERENCES IN SIGNALS

An individual child who is withdrawn or shy may also find looking at the teacher too stressful for similar reasons. For children of the same culture as the teacher, individual variation leads to different responses to the same situation. These in turn are reflected in different non-verbal behaviour, and different responses to your behaviour as teacher. Withdrawn children may encounter problems because they are over-sensitive to signals which a normal child would ignore, or because their uncertainty leads them to send inappropriate signals of stress. On the other hand, disruptive children seem to be poor at picking up early-warning signals which indicate potential confrontation with the teacher. They therefore unexpectedly find themselves in a full-blown confrontation, which a normal child would probably have avoided. From their point of view the confrontation may be unjustified, and they may react accordingly.

This reflects the general tendency of children with special needs to develop non-verbal skills more slowly than normal children. You may find that special needs children continue into their teens to take ironic statements literally, whereas only the youngest normal schoolchildren would do this. By the secondary years normal children use the non-verbal components of the message to go beyond the literal meaning of the verbal components. However, special needs children react similarly to normal children to changes in classroom layout from tables to rows (Chapter 3) and to the controlling use of touch (Chapter 9). Overall, there are likely to be considerable individual differences in the ways children with special needs react to non-verbal signals. These differences will be of two types. Firstly, there are the delays in development mentioned above. Secondly there are specific differences in sensitivity. Sensitivity may be reduced, as for the disruptive children mentioned above; or it may be increased, as for autistic children. These are hyper-sensitive to social contact; they therefore react to normal social contact in the same way as normal children would react to hostile contact. Attempts to get them to respond by normal tactics such as looking at the teacher merely increase their aversion; they are more likely to respond if an adult approaches them but does not attempt to make contact by looking at them or talking to them. In these cases children's responses are not totally outside the range of behaviour which normal children would show under extreme conditions; they merely produce them in contexts which reflect their abnormal understanding of the situation.

SEX DIFFERENCES IN SIGNALS

With the exception of some courtship signals (discussed in Chapter 9) both sexes use the same range of signals (with a few trivial differences in adults due to body structure e.g. in the way the legs are crossed). Most of our coverage, therefore, refers to children and teachers of either sex. Males tend to be more assertive than females, and some signals which tend to be thought of as male are assertiveness signals which are shown by both sexes, though more commonly by males. Similarly, females tend to use more sociable signals, such as smiling, but this again is a difference only in frequency.

SUMMARY

This chapter summarises the non-verbal channels available and the messages sent through each. Three broad types of message are sent through non-verbal signals, the most important being messages identifying feelings, both positive and negative. These feelings can be about interpersonal relationships, such as praise, interest or criticism, or about the subject matter of the lesson. Positive and negative feelings are conveyed mainly by facial expressions, but secondarily by some types of intonation (such as wait time) and gesture, and head and body posture. The second group of messages, related to the first, is about the intensity of feeling or involvement. Greater intensity is signalled by increased gaze and proximity, though other signals such as speech volume are used. For example, both intense criticism and intense praise would be signalled by sustained gaze, but they would be distinguished by the facial expression used. The final group of non-verbal messages supplement the meaning of speech; either by taking over part of the message or by indicating how it is structured and can be decoded. Most gestures and the intonation patterns of speech fall into this group.

The exercises allow you to assess how much your existing knowledge of non-verbal signals allows you to judge intentions – both as isolated signals and as signals in context.

TRAINING MATERIALS

How much do we know already?

We have found that a common reaction when discussing non-verbal communication with teachers is their tendency to dismiss much of it as 'psychobabble' or, worse still, as descriptive inventions used to turn non-events into deeply significant ones! The extent to which you can rely on non-verbal communication as a reliable classroom tool will depend as much on your own reaction as anything else.

Research suggests that non-verbal communication can account for up to 80 per cent of impression conveyed and that most of us are already aware of much of its meaning by the time we are five, and reach an adult level of skill by the age of twelve to fourteen.

As a somewhat light-hearted introduction, consider your immediate reactions to the following images – images that cannot be coloured by the spoken word!

Pictorial Exercise – 'Cat Pictures'

Question 1   Which animal would you be prepared to approach ?

Question 2   Perhaps, more significantly, if you had to make an approach, how would it vary with each display?

Clearly these considerations have little to do with classroom situations, but they do illustrate a point, namely that we are all able to read non-verbal images in such a way that we form opinions and react accordingly.

Applying these thoughts to the human field, the following exercise serves to illustrate the power behind some of the more obvious stances taken by our pupils. Avid followers of 'tough guy' movies may instantly recognise some of these stereotypes!

Single figure stances

Question 1   What is your assessment of each of the boys in Figures 2.4–2.6?

Question 2   Images can, on occasions, be as ambiguous as the spoken word. Take the stances depicted in Figures 2.7–2.9, for example, and make an assessment of what you feel each could be saying and to what extent they are likely to present a potential threat to your classroom control. They may be sending conflicting messages, so what else is needed if the image is to be more clearly understood?

Figure 2.1

Figure 2.2

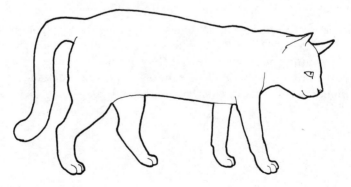

Figure 2.3

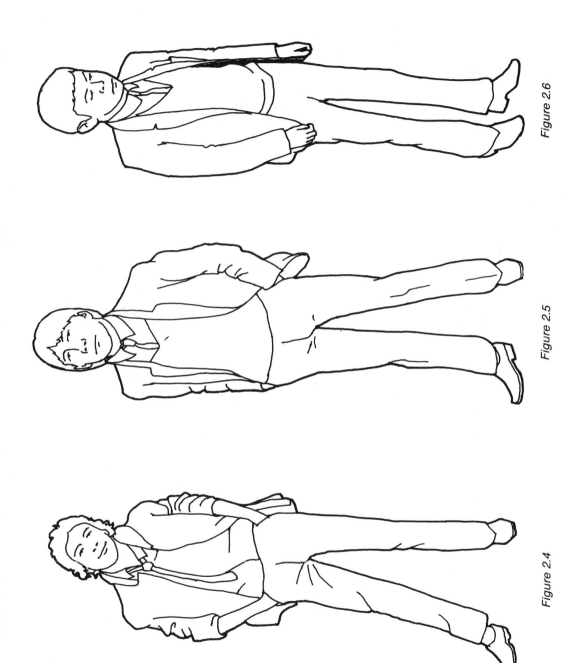

Figure 2.6

Figure 2.5

Figure 2.4

Figure 2.7

Figure 2.8

Figure 2.9

Descriptive Exercise – 'Using your knowledge'

It is important at the outset to examine the breadth of your existing knowledge and understanding. Try using the exercises below to survey your existing skills. The situations outlined may be familiar to you. If you have the opportunity, discuss your reactions with others and, if it helps, develop the situations by linking them to events that you have encountered personally.

Situation 1
Jon and Ian are late for their lesson. They have just had break on the field, which they spent together, and have arrived in a somewhat dishevelled state, ties undone, shirt tails out and chewing gum.

Mrs Powerhouse, an experienced teacher, has been concerned with their behaviour and attitude for some time and in particular the effect that they have been having on the remainder of her class. On their arrival she set about restoring the balance of power in the following manner.

She asked to see them both outside the classroom, placing Jon some way up the corridor out of earshot. She then spoke to Ian: 'Look at me, Ian. Take your hands out of your pockets, do up your tie and stand up straight. Are you chewing? Well take it out and hold it; you can put it in the bin later.'

She spent some minutes explaining her concern, on a number of occasions reminding Ian to face her. She then ended by saying, 'Now let's assume that this is all past history and start again. Go in now and get your work out.'

During the whole incident she kept her eyes fixed on Ian, but as he returned to the classroom she placed a friendly hand on his shoulder as he passed. Mrs Powerhouse then turned her attention to Jon. 'Right', she said, 'come here lad. Did you hear any of that? Well I'm sure that you can guess what it was about . . .'.

The repeat performance over, all returned to the lesson and worked productively.

This sort of situation occurs every day in schools, at all levels and ages, but why did Mrs Powerhouse deal with it in that way?

Question 1   Why did she remove them from the room first? What may have been their reaction if they had remained? How could this have affected the remainder of the class?

Question 2   As she spoke to the boys, she made them change their posture. Why did she do this, and why is it generally so successful?

Question 3   Why did she separate the boys when she began talking to them? What effect would this have had on the one waiting?

Question 4   It may have been a successful ploy on this occasion, but leaving a class in order to deal with miscreants can be a dangerous gamble, especially for the less experienced teacher. Can you suggest ways in which she could have dealt with the situation inside the classroom and still have retained her power and status?

TRAINING MATERIALS — ANSWERS TO EXERCISES

Figure 2.1   This posture is what most people think of as an 'angry' cat. However, the threat posture is a mixture of aggression (shown by the arched back and bottle-brush tail, which make the animal look larger and more formidable) and fear (shown especially in the face and ears). This cat will probably retreat, if approached boldly. The vital point to notice is that angry threat indicates an element of fear; thus if you shout at a class you are conveying some degree of fear of them.

Figure 2.2   Fearful threat, shown by a cornered cat. The head is similar to 2.1 and the hunched posture is non-threatening. An animal in this posture would fight back only if attacked, but 'feels' itself to be in imminent danger of attack. If approached, it will flee if it can. We hope you never experience this degree of fear in the classroom, but there are less extreme versions (e.g. Figure 7.16).

Figure 2.3   Dominant cat, which will attack readily if its opponent does not retreat. If approached by a person, it may become more fearful (Figure 2.1). This posture differs from a relaxed posture mainly in the steady gaze and rather deliberate, 'walking tall' gait. The two main points are willingness to act at once, and calm lack of defensiveness.

Figure 2.4   A cheerful extrovert at a school with a uniform, who was photographed demonstrating adjustments to this uniform illustrating typical forms of adaptation and exaggeration. His alterations to the styling of his clothing show both awareness of the then current fashion style and the self-confidence necessary to wear it like this. Such an overt display as this would clearly be appreciated by his peers. The relaxed, nonchalant stance, with all his weight transferred to one hip, hands resting loosely in pockets and head tilted to one side, indicates the level of confidence necessary to deal with a low-level challenge from the teacher. Handled correctly, however, he should not represent a high risk. Many experienced teachers would avoid a challenge here, or at least couch their challenge in humour; given jocular recognition and having made his point, the boy will probably be happy to readjust his clothing.

Figure 2.5   Here we have the potential for trouble. The aggressive stance, arms drawn back, coupled with the raised jaw and fixed stare, all suggest that this character is ready for conflict. The problem may have been caused elsewhere, but is potentially difficult for the current teacher to deal with. Later chapters will suggest how to defuse a situation like this, but the first and most important rule must be for the teacher to avoid echoing any of these signals; to do so would be to invite confrontation.

Figure 2.6   There is little sign of potential conflict here. This character is showing all the signs of submission and defeat, indeed, it may be as much as the teacher can do to regenerate this pupil's confidence. The downcast face, lowered shoulders and loose arm position all signal a pupil who has no stomach for conflict. This is not to say, however, that he will not become part of a difficult situation, particularly if he is allowed to become prey to peer-barracking because of perceived weakness.

Figure 2.7   Joint gaze and conversation accompany attention directed to the work; note their orientation towards each other, shutting out communication from outside. If cooperation has been specifically forbidden, this could be a challenge, though their relaxed postures suggest not. Such cooperation is likely to happen anyway, and the prudent teacher will avoid making a challenge of it wherever possible.

Figure 2.8 An 'interaction set' (the boy facing away from you is acting as the boundary of the group) waiting for the start of a lesson. Rough-and-tumble barging and chewing uniform are likely to be against the rules of most schools; their direction of gaze indicates that the boy on the right is monitoring what the reaction will be. The boy in the centre indicates the importance of accurate and speedy reaction. His apparently threatening moves are in fact flinching away from a strike from the boy on the left. In avoiding this attack he bumped into the boy on the right, who counter-attacked him. An inexperienced teacher might easily punish him for his apparently offensive behaviour, when he is in fact the weakest member of the group.

Figure 2.9 This image may make you wonder what you have said, either because you perceive this as a pupil who is totally absorbed or, alternatively, one on the point of a nervous breakdown. The stare, coupled with a neutral expression and furrowed brow, are commonly seen in people in a state of deep concentration, when reading a book, for example. The arm hold, however, seems to indicate a level of anxiety. This picture is ambiguous in this respect and is difficult to read out of the context from which it was taken, but give yourself a point if you read both interpretations!

Descriptive Exercise – 'Using your knowledge'

Question 1
Mrs Powerhouse's decision to remove both pupils from the room was an astute move. Not only did it have the effect of isolating them from their peers and removing the possibility of visual and verbal back-up (smiling, laughing, etc.), but it also left the class in the dark as to how she was using her authority and removed the possibility of her exposing her weakness if she had failed to have any effect on the offenders.

Question 2
Adopting a specific postural attitude when speaking to the boys was another successful tactic. She took the first boy through a series of status-reducing exerices; standing straight, removing hands from pockets, and insisting on eye contact is an excellent way of showing that you hold the status to do these things and, in the process, strips the pupil of his assumed power. In normal social interactions equality is signalled by neither side having the right to comment on the other's non-verbal postures. Assuming that right indicates a clear hierarchy. If we think of the situation within the Armed Forces, this is a common exercise with new recruits when establishing the chain of command. Particularly powerful in this approach is the making and maintenance of eye contact. Pupils who are low in status will find eye contact from the teacher unnerving, as they know it has no affectionate interpretation and must therefore reflect the opposite.

Question 3
Separating the boys was yet another useful ploy. By distancing one pupil she was

exercising her authority in showing that she has the power to do this. In addition the boy is placed at a distance from which he is unable to follow the conversation. He has no alternative but to use his imagination, and seeing his friend being stripped of his challenge will only serve to reduce his own.

Question 4
No matter how much authority you hold over a class, leaving them, even for a moment, can be a risky business. To deal with this problem equally effectively in the classroom she would have had to have separated the boys in some way, keeping them at the front of the room, facing her and so that they were isolated from any sympathetic or reinforcing gestures, particularly eye contact with their peers. The alternative would have been to allow them to take their place in the room and go to them *in situ*, ideally speaking to them from behind, after ensuring that the remainder of the class are busily engaged on the task at hand. To make this approach really successful she would have needed to whisper, thereby giving the opportunity to move in close to the boys, invading their personal space and adding a further measure of discomfort, to reinforce the message.

Chapter 3

Stage directions and props

Some aspects of non-verbal communication, in its broadest sense, can be arranged before the lesson starts. These include the layout of the room, which can influence communication with the class in general or with specific children, and dress cues, which both teacher and children can use as a fixed signal to everybody they encounter of the kind of person they would like to be taken as. These factors have the enormous advantage that you can arrange them with time to reflect and if necessary to consult colleagues: unfortunately their effect is not strong enough to overcome disastrous execution during the lesson itself.

Goffman's (1972) 'dramaturgical' view of social interaction – that in front of an audience social actors perform roles which may differ sharply from their private behaviour – applies very obviously to the old-style formal classroom, where the teacher is actually raised on a dais in front of her audience, but is appropriate to all classrooms. For instance, Delamont (1976) describes the way in which established teachers with their own teaching bases were able to present their own personality and view of their subject by their room displays of books, apparatus or pictures. By contrast, new teachers were shown to be marginal members of the staff by having no base in their subject area, so they often had to move round like the children, with no right to control the environment of their classroom. (One of us recalls teaching science in an ordinary classroom with no gas or water as a triumph of improvisation over curriculum which did not greatly impress the classes he taught.) In many schools, of course, this segregation between the established and the novice is not displayed in the same way, as all teachers move from room to room, though specialist subject rooms serve as discipline-specific settings.

THE EFFECTS OF SEATING ARRANGEMENT

Seating arrangements such as a circle or horseshoe of chairs are often suggested for lessons where everybody in the class is actively involved, for instance discussions, music, or language work. Here the seating arrangement and positioning of the children is being used to convey an expectation of the lesson process, and you will often move the furniture between or within lessons to fit the work you plan to do. (Incidentally, your right to rearrange the furniture again indicates your superior status relative to the class.) By contrast, primary teachers both in England and Australia, who felt they had had open-plan schools imposed on them, restored the more formal arrangement they preferred by arranging desks to face them, using cupboards to wall off their area and limiting children's freedom of movement to areas over which they could maintain effective surveillance.

Classroom arrangements designed to facilitate particular kinds of class interaction are a 'fossilized' example of the way social interaction is influenced by distance. Hall's (1966) pioneering book pointed out that people space themselves out in characteristic ways in normal interaction. Though subsequent work has shown that things are much more complex than Hall's original classification scheme suggests, it is still useful as a means for organising our thinking. Hall termed the normal spacing of two to five feet, which people adopt when talking to friends or acquaintances, sitting or standing, 'social distance'. Teachers are likely to sit or stand at this distance in the staffroom; children will adopt 'social distance' in the playground or classroom when talking to each other, and it is the distance to which children will approach when they are talking to you in the corridor or at your desk or table. People who are closer than this, in 'personal distance', run the risk of bumping each other accidentally, and unless they have an intimate relationship, they tend to move further apart. (Secondary pupils may use personal distance subversively, as discussed in Chapter 9.)

Personal distance increases as children get older. Young children are much more inclined to stand close to each other or to adults, and they are more willing to touch or be touched by them (Chapter 9). Because of its implication of intimacy, personal distance intensifies any conversation where it is used, whether aggressive, assertive, or helpful and friendly (Chapter 9). One sign of your control over the classroom is that you always have freedom of movement so you can adjust your distance from children and invade their personal distance if you want to, whereas you often deny them freedom of movement.

Without indulging in a disgraceful scrum, there is no way in which a class of thirty can all be within social distance of the teacher; many must fall outside this range, into Hall's (1966) 'public distance' (Figure 3.1). At this distance a more measured and less subtle type of communication becomes necessary. This is very clear in large open spaces such as playing fields, but the influence is already apparent in the ordinary classroom. People who want to hold an ordinary conversation cannot easily do so at public distance and have to move to social distance, but the constraints of public distance are no problem when talk is directed at a group in general, rather than a specific individual.

The effects of distance do not apply equally to all members of the class; children are inevitably at different distances. If you spend much of the lesson near your blackboard

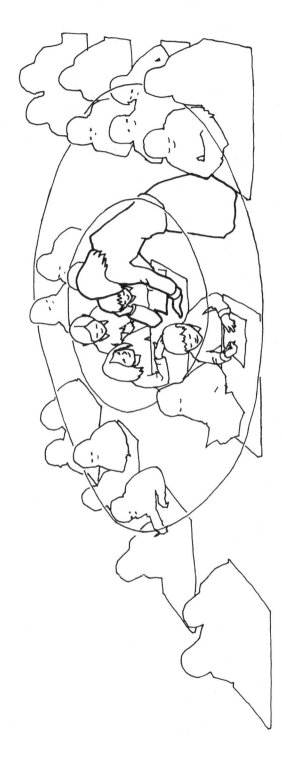

Figure 3.1 Personal, social and public distance as the teacher moves round the classroom (cf. Figure 9.3). Her behaviour will have particularly strong effects on the children within personal distance, but she will be more easily able to influence children within social distance with lower-intensity behaviour than the rest of the class

or desk, a child in the front row of the classroom may usually be at a social distance from you, while one at the back will seldom be out of public distance. Research since the 1920s has suggested that classrooms contain an 'action zone' where the teacher directs most of her attention and from which most of the class response comes. That some children receive vastly more attention from the teacher than others has been well documented; as we shall see in Chapter 7, this is probably inevitable. However, Adams and Biddle (1970) claimed that in a conventional classroom, with the teacher at centre front, her attention was concentrated on children in a kite-shaped area in the centre of the classroom. Those at the rear corners of the classroom got little attention; this is relatively easily related to their distance from the teacher. At first it seems puzzling that those at the front corners of the classroom also got little attention, but observations on university seminars provide an explanation. Students or children out of the teacher's main line of sight (in this case those sitting at the ends of a table on either side of the teacher) are effectively 'further' from her than those who are constantly under her eye; being looked at only occasionally from a close distance is equivalent to being looked at often from further away! Classroom folklore confirms the semi-immunity of the seats which are literally 'beneath the teacher's notice'.

Subsequent research has indicated that Adams and Biddle's 'kite' is rather idealised, and that the distribution of attention, while always uneven, can take different shapes, depending on the layout of the classroom, the subject being taught, and, no doubt, the particular children being taught and the cliques they fall into.

Seating position and lesson involvement – cause or effect?

A critical question is whether children choose seats to reflect their behaviour, or whether seating position itself determines behaviour. Obviously if behaviour can be affected by seating position, you are offered a control technique which does not, like most others, depend on constant vigilance to detect second-by-second changes in children's behaviour. This assumes, of course, that you are teaching in a school where you have a legitimate right to control children's seating position – if there is a formal or informal rule that children can control their own seats, your efforts may be resented and resisted. There is a widespread feeling among teachers that arranging children in suitable groups and moving them to enforce discipline are effective techniques. While moving children around is potentially a useful tactic, in most classrooms it needs to be applied with discretion. As an obvious controlling tactic, it is likely to be resented or resisted if you move children once trouble has occurred, from established positions they have chosen themselves.

A general awareness of where potential trouble-makers are likely to base themselves, and the ability to show decisiveness in dealing with them, may serve you better. For example, Ms Hola, a Spanish teacher in our videotape recordings, in her first oral lesson immediately but pleasantly moved a group of boys out of a huddle half behind the storage heater in the back corner of the classroom. This was in her first couple of minutes' contact with the class and before finding out whether these were the trouble-makers. She thus gave herself the chance to start getting the interest of the subject and her enthusiasm for it across in a quiet and receptive atmosphere, having already demonstrated that she had control of the classroom (the successful progress of this lesson is dealt with in Chapter 5). As another example, Mr Weathering's first move was to tell his class they could sit where they liked, his second to tell them they could take their jackets off, as it was a hot day (clothes are discussed in more detail below). He thus *gave permission* for them to choose, indicating at once that he had the right to control these aspects of their behaviour, and that he was a sympathetic person. If he had left the class to make their own decisions with no previous word, he would have started to lose the initiative, as anything he then said would have been a reaction to actions they had already taken. We will meet him again in Chapters 7 and 8.

In more formal schools, you may usefully be able to arrange children in alphabetical order at this stage in the school year, as Marland (1975) suggests, perhaps disguising your true intentions by telling them that this will make it much easier for you to learn their names. You then have the opportunity to show your benevolence later in the year by relaxing your control over the seating arrangements.

The little research evidence on seating position which is available is somewhat equivocal. Macpherson (1983), working in Australian secondary schools, found that the most dominant and disruptive children in the class chose their own seating positions so as to be as far as possible from the teacher. Middle-ranking children sat between them and the teacher, with the lowest-ranking (and most work-oriented) children closest to her. (As the teacher was based in one corner of the classroom, the 'hostile tribes' were concentrated in the other corner.) When the teacher countered this arrangement by moving to the back corner opposite her desk and doing as much of her teaching as possible from there, the seating arrangement suddenly reversed itself. The dominant children took over the previously despised seats by the teacher's desk, driving the least powerful members of the class to the back corner, so they were once more under the teacher's eye. Here, clearly, seating arrangements reflected children's relative ability to control their interaction with the teacher.

A rather different picture emerges from Schwebel and Cherlin (1972), working with primary children. When children's seats were swapped by the experimenters, children who were moved forward worked more and were rated as more attentive and likeable by their teachers. One explanation may be that once children learn what the reputations of particular classroom positions are, they have to live up to their position in classroom society, whether they chose it for themselves or had it chosen for them. This may apply more to younger children; work with students suggests that by this age, individuals have strong preferences and resist attempts to change their style, whether they are active participants who normally choose central seats, or low participants who choose peripheral seats.

Schwebel and Cherlin's study suggests that the effect of seating position may be as much on the teacher's perception of children and her expectations of them as on the children's actual behaviour. There is some evidence for this from a similar study by Moore and Glynn (1984) on primary children in New Guinea; when a child to whom the teacher addressed many questions swapped seats with one to whom she addressed fewer, their subsequent levels of questioning reflected their new positions. Teachers, like children, get to know the reputation of particular areas of the classroom and base their responses on this knowledge.

Seating arrangements: tables and rows

We have already mentioned that not being looked at makes the child feel 'further' from you. Not facing you also makes the child feel 'further away'. The same applies to classroom arrangements with the children seated around tables, with many facing away from or sideways on to the teacher. These are typical of primary schools and almost all the research on the effects of these seating arrangements has been done at this age; but they also occur in science laboratories and other practical rooms where large tables or benches are needed to carry out the work. There is some evidence to suggest that in situations like this, moving a child who is facing away from you so that he is face-to-face can improve work and behaviour.

Available research on the effect of seating arrangement in junior schools (Wheldall and Glynn 1989 summarise this work) suggests that children's application and output of work improves when they are moved from table groups to rows, and deteriorates when they return to tables. This applies for both normal children and those with special needs. One problem here is that these studies were short-term (a week or two with each arrangement) and the differences may mainly reflect the novelty of the seating change. However, similar studies of mixed and single-sex groups found that juniors worked better in mixed-sex groups, whether these were an experimental novelty or their usual seating pattern – in other words, moving children who normally worked in mixed pairs to segregated seating led to a decrease in performance. The opposite effect occurred with secondary pupils. This reflects the change in children's preferences from same-sex to mixed-sex informal groupings with age.

When we remember the importance of peer relations to children, it is likely that children will take the opportunity to talk to each other if the layout permits it, and seating across a typically sized table is the best position for conversation (Sommer 1969)! People of all ages prefer to face each other to talk, and a table places them at the distance they would normally choose if they had freedom of movement. Obviously you can hope that this conversation will be about the work, but you will have to produce stimulating work to ensure that this is so; even then you will probably have to keep a careful eye on proceedings. Bennett, Desforges *et al.*'s (1984) work in infant classrooms suggests that children's genuine attempts to help each other can often have very limited value, simply because by definition they have not yet achieved a full grasp of the curriculum area they are dealing with, and the blind tend to lead the blind astray. This effect will probably occur at any age, though as children become more critical and more aware of the deficiencies of their own knowledge, they may be more cautious in offering advice. Older children are also much more aware of the relative cleverness of different members of the class, and will probably temper their acceptance of suggestions by their knowledge of the source. Bossert (1979) found that in classes where emphasis was placed on academic performance, children would only sit with others of similar ability, probably for this reason.

Seating positions also provide an informal sociogram. Our own experience is that it is possible to predict the children who will make mutual choices on a sociogram by looking at how children arrange themselves when they are free to sit where they like. Seating choice will fit friendship patterns more accurately for high-status members of the class, who will displace low-status members and isolates: this is fortunate, as the higher-status ones are more likely to cause you classroom management problems. As long ago as 1966 it was found that American college students' prejudices relating to sex and race were reflected in the way they segregated themselves in the classroom. When prejudice lessened, so did segregation. There is a similar tendency to segregate into clusters in dining-hall queues and the playground.

Actual choice of seat is a relatively static index of feelings, but, as we shall see in Chapters 5 and 9, children show their degree of involvement on a moment-to-moment basis by mutual orientation and eye contact. Streeck (1983) analysed in detail a mixed-sex group of seven to nine-year-olds. One child had been given a task by the teacher and had to get the rest to carry it out. When the children were working as a group they formed one cluster; if they were all listening to one child, all turned to focus on her, while if they had split into pairs to work the pairs oriented towards each other, cutting off other members of the group (these patterns are illustrated in the exercises for Chapter 5). The teacher's assignment of a leadership role to one child sometimes differed from the children's existing hierarchy, and then, especially, much of their time was spent sorting out who was in charge. The course of these arguments was clearly reflected in their postures. When the task was finished the group as a whole would 'open up' to the outside world by leaning back in their chairs and looking round. Seating postures and arrangements offer useful cues which you can use to check what is going on from across the room; they can be taken in relatively quickly and you do not have to be able to hear what members of the group are saying to get a general picture of their level of cooperation and involvement with their work.

COSTUMING THE STAGE: THE MESSAGES OF DRESS

You will be well aware of your own need to 'dress for the part'; you are unlikely to have got where you are unless you have been appropriately dressed for your interviews. Most schools have unstated norms of staff dress. If as a new teacher you are going to have to rely for support or assistance from your colleagues, you are probably well advised to dress as 'one of the team', as seen through the eyes of the children.

Children themselves, as we have already implied, are especially 'team-conscious' in the early secondary years and keeping up-to-date with whatever is the current 'everybody's wearing it' is one of the major crosses borne by their parents. For example, among football supporters, very complex systems of meaning for different items of clothing and exactly how they are worn (for example the exact type and positioning of a scarf) can evolve (Marsh, Rosser and Harre 1978). In schools where children are allowed to come in their own choice of clothes this can become an overriding obsession. They may not wear their hearts on their sleeves, but they will probably wear their

Figure 3.2 Two twelve-year-old girls, from a 1983 class photograph in a school with no uniform. The girl on the left has tinted and styled hair, in addition to her ear-rings and clothes in the current fashion. The other, accepted by the rest of the class as its cleverest member, has more 'pre-teen' clothes and hair-style

assessment of the relative importance of in-school and out-of-school activities (Figure 3.2)!

In schools which have a uniform, the new teacher can usefully look out for the badge of the subversive, or check with established colleagues if a pattern of clothing appears to be consistently associated with those who get up to dark deeds in the back corner of the classroom and refuse to come out. If there are uniform rules, you will be expected to enforce them, and you will probably be tested on whether you can do this as soon as you meet the class. We have mentioned above the way in which Mr Weathering immediately but positively asserted his control over whether his class could wear their jackets. Many pupils gain peer status from slight manipulation of the school rules governing dress and uniform (see the exercises for Chapter 2). Pupils with such social confidence often have high influence with their peers (Caswell 1982) and tend to be acutely aware of the dangers to personal status inherent in a challenge based on a clear infringement of uniform or dress rules. Usually with this form of deviant behaviour, posture is relaxed and the child often smiles and directs conversation only to close group members, all indicating a *closed challenge*. In the next two chapters we move on to look at pupils' behaviour, and especially the extent to which it indicates a challenge to you and whether these challenges are serious *open challenges* or *closed challenges* which you can take with less concern. On the other hand, and more promisingly, pupils' behaviour *may* indicate fascinated acceptance of what you are trying to do.

SUMMARY

Classroom layout and dress are aspects of non-verbal communication which can be planned in advance to set expectations for the lesson when it starts. Distance affects the quality of interaction, and pupils who are in the centre of the classroom facing the teacher receive more attention than others. This is due both to active seat choice by pupils and differential attention by the teacher. Row seating arrangements, and mixed-sex seating, lead to higher work output for junior pupils, since they discourage social talk; but these results may not apply for secondary pupils. Short-term changes in children's seating arrangements reflect the progress of work and can be used for monitoring pupils from a distance. Dress is used by teachers, and more especially pupils, to stake a claim for the impression they wish to give in the classroom.

The excercises look firstly at how our attitudes to pupils and pupils groups are likely to be affected by the position they choose in the classroom, as well as how they form groups and behave. Secondly we discuss the effect these patterns of behaviour might have on an inexperienced colleague's class management problems.

TRAINING MATERIALS

Few of us could, with all honesty, deny that we have attended lectures, courses or even staff meetings without at some time deliberately choosing where we sat. If you recall the last time you sat at or near the back, was it by accident or design? Were you there with a specific group of colleagues? Was it that you didn't want to attend, or at least did not want to take an active part? Do you recall holding whispered conversations, reading something that had nothing to do with the meeting, or having to ask someone nearby what point on the agenda had been reached? The fact is that where we sit and who we sit with does have a direct bearing on our active involvement with the task in hand, even as professional and responsible adults and even if we have volunteered to be there!

So how much more significant it must be to a group of children who, amazingly, may not wish to be 'there' in the classroom.

Pictorial Exercise: 'Who calls the tune?'

The first exercise attempts to examine the tendency we have to change our assumptions as to a pupil or pupils' intent, according to where they are sitting in the room.

Figure 3.3   Assuming for the moment that the classroom seating arrangement is fairly fixed (perhaps this is a lesson taught in another teacher's room and you do not wish to disturb things), examine the situations outlined below and consider your reactions.

Question 1   If this were happening at the rear of the classroom, some distance from you, how would you view it?

Question 2   If it occurred within the group immediately in front of you, would you feel the same?

Question 3   What are the signs that something positive is taking place?

Question 4   Are there any potentially negative signs?

Figure 3.4   With the second picture, consider how you could impose your authority on the group by changing the props; in this case theirs!

Question 5   Does this picture suggest to you that this group is likely to be disruptive?

Question 6   In what ways could you suggest changing the situation to increase your status and authority, but without causing unnecessary antagonism?

Figure 3.5   It is equally important when setting your stage to assess the condition of the players as and when they arrive. By watching them carefully it is often possible to draw conclusions as to where the potential problems lie and whether to adjust the set accordingly. We look at this problem in the third picture.

Here we have a number of pupils arriving together.

Question 7   Place them in order of concern and try to identify the root cause of your uneasiness.

Question 8   Would you allow them to sit together? If so, where and what limitations, if any, would you place upon them?

Figure 3.3

Figure 3.4

Figure 3.5

Descriptive Exercise - 'Giving an inch'

Miss Newton, a teacher of Science, has found herself having to teach one period per week of History to a class of fifteen-year-olds. She has not long been at the school and has not had time to become a recognised member of the school staff in the eyes of the children. Her first few lessons with this class went reasonably well. She had prepared their work meticulously and she felt that they seemed interested.

After a time, however, she found that the class were forming themselves into groups or cliques within the classroom. At the same time they began to pay less and less attention to her, were often not listening, and began to act in a number of devious and disruptive ways.

By half term, she found that she was dreading the lesson and became more and more concerned at facing this particular group. She soon realised that she had to take action. She took the time to discuss the situation with a colleague and described the way in which she approached the lesson. This is a summary:

I am always in the room when they arrive. As they come in I stand at the front and try to direct them to sit near me where there are spare spaces. Always, however, a number, and I know in advance which they will be, sit at the back. When I ask them to move they stare directly at me in an intimidating way and say 'Why? We haven't done anything.' I always make sure that a monitor hands out the books and equipment, so that I can keep an eye on the class at all times, picking them up every time something is said or implied. Recently things have got worse, and last week they would not stop talking or even listen to instructions at the start of the lesson. I am not sure what I am doing, but I do know that they can sense that I am bothered by them and even a little nervous of them.

Question 1   From Miss Newton's description of her lesson, how would you imagine that she is coming across to this class? What non-verbal signals would you ask her if she was displaying?

Question 2   What could she do to re-establish her status and authority with this group, and how could she deal with the pupils who have formed themselves into a clique?

TRAINING MATERIALS — ANSWERS TO EXERCISES

Figure 3.3 This image was taken from a Drama lesson where pupils were preparing an improvisation. The mood of the lesson was relaxed, but productive, on the whole. Making judgements of a group of pupils is always difficult, particularly a large group like this one. However, the tendency here, if viewed from afar, may be to assume at first sight that little is being achieved. Clearly, at the point of illustration only one or two pupils are actively engaged in discussion. This is characteristic of conversational groups of any type but it would be difficult, if this was happening at the rear of the room, to say if this discussion was in any way productive.

There are positive signs here, however; signs that the group is working on a task. The gaze of all group members is specific in direction and focused on one pupil (the boy, front left). The forward lean shown by the group members indicates interest in the conversation and there is no attempt to block the view of the teacher or to check on her presence. The group at this stage do not represent a direct challenge to her authority.

If there are any potential concerns they centre on the boy, whose relaxed, almost nonchalant pose indicates high status within the class and is echoed in the response of the remainder of the group. Additional concern may arise from the fact that he is leaning back from a group forward of the illustration and may, therefore, have little legitimate cause to be holding audience in the first place. As teacher, you might wish to move unobtrusively closer to get a chance of hearing whether he is making a highly constructive contribution to the development of ideas in their group, minding their business rather than his own, or swapping impressions of last night's soap.

Figure 3.4 Changing props is, when appropriate, an excellent way of confirming or imposing authority. Here we have a breakaway couple taken from the same Drama lesson as Figure 3.3. The diversion from task is confined to the two pupils front right, as the remainder of the group are still clearly intent on the task. The boy's backward lean and clutching of the girl's chair and their mutual smile and gaze indicate an involvement with each other, rather than with the task at hand!

The behaviour is still quite closed, however, and confined to the pupils concerned, both facts suggesting little attempt to erode the teacher's authority. Even so, it is important to guide them back to task before their behaviour forms a precedent and erodes the involvement of the whole group. Authority can be established by gently reminding them of the task, and asking them to return to their original seating arrangement. Further effect could be achieved by insisting in the boy's case that he remove his outer coat and mittens to comply with the school dress regulations. If these 'reminders' are given in a matter-of-fact way they often serve to illustrate the power base of the teacher without becoming antagonistic, particularly if they are done with a smile and low-level humour.

Figure 3.5 This group happens to be male, although they belong to a coeducational school. The very fact that they have arrived together and are so clearly absorbed in each other says much about their mutual social confidence. Thoughts about the value of the forthcoming lesson are probably far from their minds. If you feel uneasy about this group your thoughts may centre around the 'physical' nature of their behaviour.

Boy 'A' (facing away) is dominant within this group, and engaged in a playful encounter with pupil 'B' (eyes shut). We can describe the encounter as 'playful' as pupil 'C' (left) is also interfering with pupil 'A'. This situation would not occur if pupil 'A' were displaying aggressive signals, as most peripheral pupils instinctively back away from potential violence.

Boy 'D' (foreground) is detached from this group, however, and his solitary behaviour may signal not only his lack of enthusiasm for the next lesson in the short term. If sustained it indicates his emotional, almost 'moody' detachment from the group as a whole. The approach of pupils 'A' and 'D' seem poles apart at this stage and it would seem prudent to keep them apart during the lesson. The others will probably end their fun and games once the lesson begins, but it would be worth mentioning that you have noticed their 'high spirits' and will be keeping an eye on them.

Descriptive Exercise - 'Giving an inch'

Question 1

Clearly Miss Newton is sending signals that are having the effect of eroding her authority over a period of time. From her description it is clear that she fears this particular group. As she stands in front of the class she clearly does not display the relaxed posture of someone in control. Directing them to their chairs, and her attempt to move certain individuals to the front, draws attention to this. Their response to this request shows that they believe that she is expecting trouble.

Having equipment handed out by a monitor is a perfectly acceptable activity; but operating on the basis of scanning or watching pupils whilst this is being done, particularly in a way which implies the teacher is watching the 'hostile tribes', will erode any measure of trust that she may have had with the group and again illustrate to the class that she is uncertain of her power base. Also the notion of 'picking up' children every time something is said or implied is only likely to lead to irritation, or a sense that she is trying to 'get at' them. In any classroom a small amount of deviance will take place, but where this does not amount to a direct and open challenge to your authority you can afford to ignore it or, at the very most, correct it with a fair measure of light-hearted and relaxed humour.

Things may have got worse largely because the class will have seen themselves as being punished for something that they hadn't even done. They may feel that she has fired all her guns, and they cerainly know that she is unsure of herself. The more anxious she becomes, the further she will move from her position of authority.

Question 2

Miss Newton is already aware of the authority systems at her disposal. She is aware, for example, that she can direct pupils to sit in certain places, to appoint monitors to issue books, and to expect a measure of task-oriented activity during the lesson. High status teachers, however, are relaxed and show confidence in the way they use this authority. They confidently move around the room, they sit in a relaxed way and do not continually refer to notes. They let certain issues go, particularly if they do not perceive them as a threat, but they are prepared to invade their pupils' personal space and use dominance displays when necessary.

The first step Miss Newton could take to re-establish her status would be to distance herself from her pedantic adherence to minor rules. A more relaxed approach to the pupils, particularly as they enter the class, coupled with an 'apparent' indifference to their seating arrangements would considerably improve her situation. Smiling, involving the pupils in domestic discussions, sitting on the desk rather than using it as a protective barrier, all these are simple moves that she can make to convince the class that she is indeed in command of her situation. With regard to the clique, she would do well to move around the room more often, perhaps teaching from the back of the room occasionally, invading the personal space of those she suspects of ignoring her instructions. Picking up exercise books without first requesting permission and checking that the work is being completed, reading over a child's shoulder from behind, involving the reluctant in discussions, are all moves which indicate she has freedom of movement and initiative. It is important to carry out these activities while maintaining a sense of low threat and humour.

If she felt it necessary, she could hold back the clique at the end of the lesson, something which she has the formal authority to do, and explain that she is unhappy with their attitude and level of work and give them the option to modify their seating arrangements or face the consequences of their actions. If this is done in a quiet voice, with deliberate and paced speech whilst holding slightly longer than average eye contact with each in turn, then her authority should once again be recognised. One word of warning, however. These suggestions, as with all changes in approach towards a class, must evolve over a period of time. To introduce such a radical change in approach might suggest to the pupils that she is trying to become too friendly, even 'pally', and they are likely to treat this with distrust and a total lack of respect.

Chapter 4

Pupil behaviour and deviancy

RULES AND THE GENERATION OF DEVIANCY

Schools provide the setting in which a great deal of childhood learning takes place. Learning, unfortunately, is not confined to academic knowledge: it may also include social strategies which enable pupils to test the extent of their control on other individuals, all too often the unsuspecting teacher. Deviancy represents just one element of such behaviour, but one that has far- reaching significance if you are a new or student teacher.

To operate effectively, a classroom must be governed by rules which in the final event you largely have to impose as the class teacher, even if they are not of your making. Rules are intended to inhibit the behaviour of pupils and to channel them into activities regulated by the teacher. Any alternative may be seen as deviant. Stated simply, if a rule is broken or ignored, deviancy occurs – no rules, no deviancy!

Deviancy is often considered to be a question of 'social definition' (e.g. Turner 1983). Events become deviant not through being a specific kind of act, but when you, as the teacher, or some other person define them as deviant. Thus concentrated work from a Maths textbook can be deviant – if it is done in school assembly or English. Talking about work, sharing equipment and walking around the room are more frequent examples of behaviour which would be acceptable in some circumstances but not others. Not all deviance is of this type – knocking another child unconscious is unacceptable in all contexts, inside or outside the classroom, except possibly in the boxing ring and even here there are deviant ways of performing this feat. It is not surprising that schools and teachers can exacerbate as well as reduce deviant behaviour – for example, uniform rules create their own possibilities for deviance (Chapter 3 and exercises for Chapter 2).

Many of the deviant acts which offend against specific school rules (such as doing Maths at the wrong time) fall into the class of *closed challenges*, which we describe in the next chapter, while *open challenges* (also described there) often involve actions – such as insulting the teacher – which offend against more general norms of behaviour.

Teachers can be 'deviant' too – the mirror image of pupil deviance. Pupils expect you to adhere to a number of unstated rules involving maintaining effective control, fairness, civility, showing knowledge and accuracy in your subject, and even enthusiasm. They may feel justified in imposing sanctions on you, by misbehaving or ignoring you, if you break these rules. If you continue to enforce rules which are seen by pupils as illegitimate, widespread deviance may result (Turner 1983). The implication of this is that rules and attendance to rules are negotiated. Pupils and teacher contribute to the balance of power within the classroom. You need to be able to recognise the behaviour patterns which may affect your ability to negotiate an effective balance.

A traditional source of help in guiding you in what to look for has always been the wealth of staffroom folklore, which offers a bewildering variety of systems, generated through years of accumulated experience. Often, however, such advice is of limited use as it represents the effects of one particular personality on a class or pupil and will have underlying it the style and status of that person. These may not be available to you as a young teacher.

Very often, effective teachers are quite unaware of where their magic skills lie. In fact once you have achieved a high level of skill it becomes automatic, and it is extremely difficult to work out exactly what cues or skills you use. This applies both to motor skills, such as driving a car, and to perceptive skills, such as being able to analyse a chess-playing position or a classroom scene. The various signs we point out laboriously here are picked up as second nature by skilled experienced teachers, who cannot understand why the novice cannot see. To them, deviant children give themselves away so blatantly that a placard drawing attention to the misdemeanour could hardly be more obvious. However, they may not be able to specify exactly what they pick up, and the same applies to the signals they send out. We have often found that even the most effective teachers get a shock when they see themselves on video. Often, they compare unfavourably their own copious use of gesture (one of the foundations of their success – Chapter 7) with the tictac men at the races. One particularly expert teacher we videoed later confessed that he was mystified at the speed with which classes learnt the individual characters of their teachers. It had not occurred to him that the classes only had to suss out ten or a dozen teachers whereas he had to get to know over two hundred children, and actually teach at the same time! Even Jove nods sometimes.

INITIAL ENCOUNTERS AND THE LEADERS OF THE PACK

As any experienced teacher will verify, much knowledge of a particular class, group or individual pupil can be gained from the initial moments of contact. This does not just apply to the teacher; the class are making good use of this time too (Beynon 1985).

Hence the importance of effective self-presentation from the start (Chapter 6). Experienced teachers often sense when problems are likely to arise and are only too aware of the effects of the time of day, or week, on a lesson with a particular group. Ball (1980), Caswell (1982), Macpherson (1983) and Beynon (1985) have shown that particular pupils, or groups of pupils, may influence strongly the level of control and work output in a particular lesson. Pupils can have specific roles within the class to test the limits of the teacher's control. Many teachers, both experienced and inexperienced, are aware of Ball's 'honeymoon period', during which time pupils appear to assess the apparent range and extent of control that a particular teacher possesses through her ability to build up 'case law' in response to each challenge she meets (Wragg and Wood 1984).

The threat to teacher authority may originate from only 10 per cent of the class, according to children's reports (Caswell 1982); this high-influence group hold a position of status among their peers. Videotape of these pupils indicated that their actions were directed more specifically to classroom disruption than those of the rest of the class: their disruptive behaviour was more overt and had a number of clearly recognisable features. A significant and relatively comforting factor is that, from the same reports, the majority of the classroom group does not appear to owe any allegiance to the high-influence disruptive pupils.

Videotapes often show other members of the class working away busily, in the next row to disruptive children, and this is consistent with Furlong's (1976) description of *interaction sets*. Furlong claimed that apparently stable cliques in the classroom concealed a constantly shifting pattern of alliances. At any moment children who were acting together formed an interaction set, but these sets had a dynamic rather than a static equilibrium. The set would persist only for as long as it was in its members' interests to belong. Individual children might make a bid to disrupt the classroom, but if the lesson material was interesting, or the teacher effective, they might fail to get any support and find themselves isolated from friends who would normally back them up – the interaction set shrank to one. However situations where disruptive pupils were not effectively dealt with drew in other members of the form whose behaviour had hitherto not been disruptive – in Furlong's terms the disruptive interaction set expanded to take in the whole class. For much of the time the disruptive set would contain the same few children, but the critical point here from your point of view, is that accurate detection and suitable action can influence interaction sets; if it is not worth while for children to belong to a disruptive interaction set they will leave it and join one which cooperates with you.

Peer group interaction can affect the teaching environment when children try to alter their status within the groups Furlong has described. Leadership struggles within peer associations can affect the balance of classroom control (Macpherson 1983) as pupils try to impress others by keeping the teacher under control – unless it is clearly understood by both pupils and teacher that such interference is not permissible. Such situations are implicitly understood by experienced teachers, who will frequently move to break up peer groups which they feel constitute a threat to overall classroom control, or may pre-empt such associations, for instance by seating children in alphabetical order (Marland 1975).

Effective teaching requires constant monitoring of these behavioural dynamics. This is particularly true in the new teaching styles involving active learning techniques, where the traditional stance of the teacher as the head of authority usually in one position in the classroom is replaced by her new role as adviser, constantly patrolling pupils who are working in groups, at a pace determined by their own abilities and interest. In these situations the noise level will rise and there may be much more general classroom movement, but this does not significantly alter the deviant behavioural patterns – it merely calls for more acute observation. Denscombe (1980b) describes similar problems in an 'open' secondary classroom where pupils are allowed freedom to move around and organise their own learning. Children may invent ingenious new forms of deviation from the subject-matter of the lesson, such as the over-friendliness described by Denscombe (see Chapter 9).

Experienced teachers have long recognised (Caswell 1982) that practical lessons tend to be noisier than academic ones. Opportunities for deviancy are increased by the freer working environment. Our tape analysis revealed an apparent increase in negative (non-productive) physical and verbal behaviour during practical sessions (Caswell 1982). This was characterised by slouching, leaning back on chairs, moving around, gazing, prodding and pushing other members of the class and shouting. The appearance thus created was of practical sessions being devoid of direction or productive work. This impression, however, proved to be misleading; when the tapes were re-examined to assess the time spent on actual work in both academic and practical sessions, this was found to vary very little. The difference is simply that the 'down-time' activities are more conspicuous in the practical lessons.

Why then does an increase in physical and verbal activity denote to most teachers an increase in deviancy and authority challenges? The answer in part seems to be the nature of what teachers see as constituting a challenge. Discussions with teachers revealed that most do not regard inattention as a serious form of deviancy; it does not constitute as great a threat to their authority as overt physical and verbal behaviours (Denscombe 1980a). Galton and Willcocks (1983) describe 'Easy Riders' – the large group of children who 'meet the demands of the classroom at an easy pace, sitting well back, as it were, to enjoy the ride'. They spend an eighth of their time distracted from the task in hand, while 'doing just enough to avoid the teacher's attention'. They may be disrupting their own prospects of learning, but they are not disrupting the lesson.

This was underlined when teachers were asked about pupils who, during the videorecording, were clearly not concentrating although they were causing minimal visible and verbal disturbance. Commenting on one pupil's obvious detachment one teacher observed: 'Hazel's always switched off. A bomb could explode and she would take a week to notice. It's usually best to leave her.' On another pupil's inactivity during Art, the comment was: 'It's sometimes easier to let it go. What is the point of putting their backs up? They can be much worse.'

Challenge to teacher authority, then, is is seen as overt and active disassociation from teacher-directed activities, which are substituted by pupils' own self-directed ones. This may explain why many teachers are apparently concerned about noise levels and general class conversation, particularly during their probationary year – and for that matter, why other members of staff often judge a new colleague by the noise level emanating from her room (Beynon 1985, Denscombe 1980a).

Where things do become understandably more complicated is where pupils are caught in a dilemma, involved with the need to display their own status to other members of the peer group, whilst having to work within the parameters of control that the teacher has laid down. This can be a particular problem for high-achieving pupils who still need to maintain 'face' with their peers (Turner 1983). Pupils' non-verbal behaviours are particularly useful in these situations as indications of actual and potential challenge, providing of course that they are clearly understood. There is no greater line of defence against a potential pupil challenge than for you to effectively identify it as such before the pupil concerned is able to capitalise on it.

In subsequent chapters we shall go into some detail describing the non-verbal behaviours of teachers and the way they set the parameters of control and constantly patrol their boundaries, but we must remember at the outset that many teacher actions are in response to events, signals, or even a supposed challenge from the pupils. This is not to say, however, that all pupils are engaged in this testing procedure, or that all pupil behaviours have disruption as their primary role. Indeed, most pupil behaviour in the classroom is easily recognisable as normal social discourse concerned with produc-tive and positive activity, rather than negative and disruptive activity.

You need to learn as soon as possible to recognise the nature of pupil exchanges, and, more particularly, to differentiate disruptive behaviours between those of a more benign nature and those likely to lead to serious erosion of your status. The effective teacher knows when to use her non-verbal and other skills in response to particular pupil behaviours.

In conclusion, we are suggesting that many pupil behaviours may have an ulterior motive in terms of disrupting or devaluing your authority; furthermore, that some of these are recognisable, assuming you are aware of what to look for. In order to make the recognition process easier, the challenges can be seen as falling into the two distinct patterns we mentioned above: *closed*, which are low-risk, representing little in the way of a direct challenge to your authority, and *open*, which are clearly designed to test or erode the parameters of your control. It is important to learn quickly to differentiate between the types and arrive at what Delamont (1976) refers to as a 'mutual definition of the situation' where the class knows that you know what they are up to. In the following chapter we will go into detail on the non-verbal markers of these two styles of deviant behaviour.

SUMMARY

Many challenges to teacher authority are low-level, usually actions which are not wrong in themselves, but which offend against rules such as not moving around the classroom without permission. You need to establish whether these challenges are serious and whether they are likely to spread. If you react more strongly than necessary you may convert a low-level challenge into a more serious one. Non-verbal signals are valuable clues, as pupils will usually wish to disguise their challenge and its nature.

The exercises aim to draw your attention to the cues which indicate whether a challenge is serious or not, and to start you thinking whether your reaction is likely to diminish a potential challenge or exacerbate it, both in the case of individual incidents and in the context of a complete lesson.

TRAINING MATERIALS

The question of what constitutes deviant behaviour will always be a thorny one. Most of us can recall days when we entered the staffroom bemoaning our fate at having to teach young 'Freddie', only to have a colleague tell us that they think he is wonderful or that they have never experienced any problems with him. It is at these times that we all wonder, 'Is it me?'

Certainly there is plenty of evidence to suggest that teachers can be instrumental in developing difficult situations, largely through frustration or fear, but other evidence points to an occasional lack of understanding on the part of the teacher as to which behaviours can be considered deviant and specifically aimed at disruption and which merely constitute normal social intercourse, albeit at the wrong time and the wrong place!

The exercises below should help you to look again at what you would consider to be deviant or potentially deviant behaviour and to question your reasons for feeling that way.

Pictorial Exercise – 'Real or Imagined'

Question 1   Taking Figures 4.1–4.4, consider with each whether you see the potential for disruption. Try and give reasons for your interpretation based on the visual clues on display in each picture.

You may have decided that one or more of the situations outlined above has potential for disruption, but you will also realise that your own reaction would do much to improve or exacerbate the situation.

Look at Figures 4.5 and 4.6, this time involving the teacher. Clearly in one case she is likely to raise the temperature considerably, creating as she does so a potentially volatile situation; but why?

Question 2   What are the significant differences between the two pictures?

Question 3   Is there any evidence that both parties in either of the pictures are taking a deviant line?

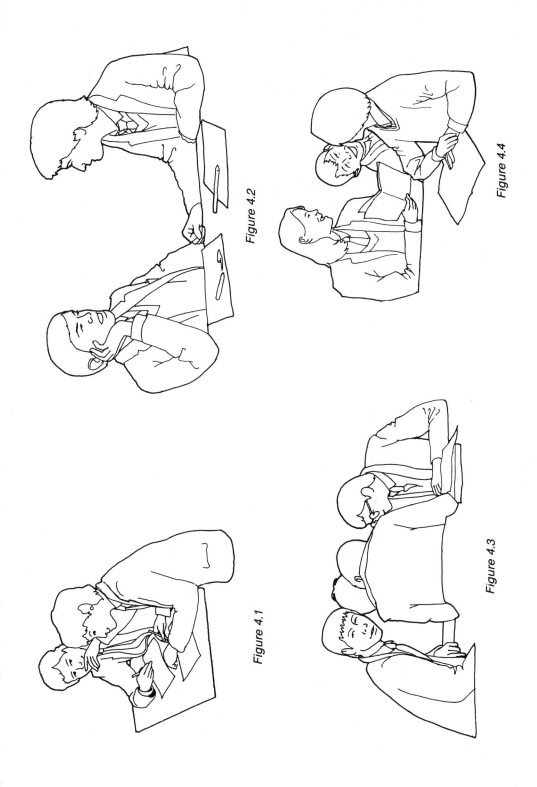

Figure 4.2

Figure 4.4

Figure 4.1

Figure 4.3

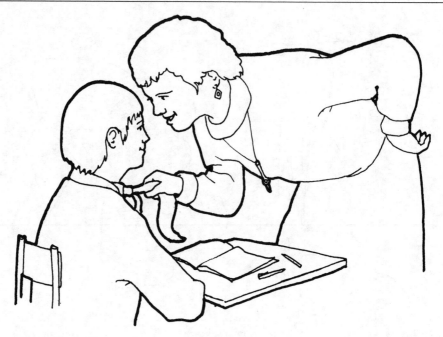

Figure 4.5

Figure 4.6

Descriptive Exercise – 'All's fair in love and war'

Mr Vangogh, a reasonably experienced teacher, is taking the class for Art and Craft. The average age of the pupils is about eleven and, as a rule, they really enjoy their Art lessons. Mr Vangogh has prepared his lesson well and they are doing practical and colourful design work using templates. The templates have been placed in large brown envelopes, about A4 size. Throughout the lesson these large envelopes have become sources of amusement, one group of three children having been playfully wearing them on their heads, rather like hats. Another particularly noisy group had been watching this millinery exercise and one of them was equally interested to see how Mr Vangogh had responded. This latter group became involved in the same game, but this time pulling them well down over their eyes and calling others in the room to see what they had done.

Mr Vangogh, who up to that point had not commented on the envelope game, believing that the class were generally working well, spoke to this latter group in severe terms, moving towards them and pointing at the individuals concerned. He accused them of disrupting his lesson and told them that if they did not desist they would stay in at break.

With this the group protested loudly that others had been doing it and had not been told off.

Question 1 What reasons do you think Mr Vangogh had for choosing to single out this particular group? What do you feel may have been the justifications present in their behaviour that were not evident in the behaviour of the others?

Question 2 Do you feel that their protests were justified and, if so, how could Mr Vangogh maintain his position without appearing to easily dismiss their claims? How can he ensure that his authority is retained without destroying the belief the class had in his ability to be fair in his treatment of them?

Question 3 Do you think that Mr Vangogh could have approached the whole lesson in a different way to ensure that this situation did not arise in the first place, or was his original judgement not to discipline the first group correct?

TRAINING MATERIALS – ANSWERS TO EXERCISES

Figure 4.1   A moment of light amusement may have broken the concentration on the task at hand, but these pupils seem to have contained the joke between themselves. The hand over mouth and the coy expressions suggest that they are aware of their deviancy, but they have not opened this up to include other members of the class. Pens in hands also suggests that their detachment is temporary. This suggests that the girls were giggling before you approached them; if they start to giggle as you approach, the situation is more threatening, for you are the source of their amusement. You will still need a light touch; they may well be looking at something illegitimate – the naughty bits of a biology textbook? – when you appeared unexpectedly. A direct, but smiling approach to find out what is so funny, establishes your right to ask, even if you do not get a very informative answer.

Figure 4.2   Here we have a conversation between two pupils who may or may not be discussing the task at hand. Their gaze is clearly mutual and their postural stance relaxed, suggesting that their activities are confined to themselves. There is no attempt to 'hide' their activities or to check for the presence of the teacher, so one suspects that they are not about to declare a mutiny!

Figure 4.3   The hunched posture of this group suggests something may be brewing. Their behaviour shows an element of concealment, indicating their wish to exclude prying eyes, especially those of the teacher. The real indicator of potential disruption is shown here in the 'flick check' of the pupil on the extreme left. This checking activity, momentary though it is, is commonly used to track the movements of the teacher, often before and after deviant acts. This type of behaviour indicates a localised open challenge and signals a group worth watching.

Figure 4.4   This is a case of concentration being interrupted. The orientation of the girl front right indicates that she has been engaged on work connected with the textbook in front of her. The position of her hands and arms shows that she has been drawn away from the task in hand by the antics of the boy behind. Her friend, on the left, has also been drawn in, the raised book acting as a fairly weak 'cover'. The closed orientation of the pupils involved indicates that this is not an open challenge to your authority, assuming that they had not already received a reminder to get on with their work and were not, therefore, deliberately creating a 'situation'. A flick check would be another indicator of an open challenge. The signs are, however, that they must be returned to the fold with firm and immediate effect if the class is to remain under your control.

Figure 4.5   Playful touch; a head-banging teacher. Teachers rarely engage in rough-and-tumble play with pupils; those who do have good relationships with their classes and are highly popular. Clearly, however, this may be a dangerous game to play. Pulling and prodding pupils, however playfully, is still technical assault and teachers who use this approach can usually be seen to display at the same time, clear and unambiguous signals of their benign intent. This particular teacher was appreciated by her class as considerate and helpful; her willingness to listen carefully to their answers in class discussion and to spend time with them when they were working individually explained this view. In the case shown here, the boy had failed to follow her instructions on how classwork should be set out; after the head-banging, she allowed him to carry on, rather than make him spoil his book by trying to correct it.

Figure 4.6   The boy's head-down posture with averted gaze indicates submission. The teacher's folded arms indicate that she is under some stress. She is clearly winning the confrontation, but the indication of stress on her part may lead to an erosion of her authority if displayed too often. The point having been made, she would do well to soften her line with the pupil concerned after returning him to his desk, in order to strengthen her authority and show that she can behave in a relaxed way. Children saw this teacher as 'strict', or 'serious' – both types they would tend to avoid.

Descriptive Exercise – 'All's fair in love and war'

Question 1
Mr Vangogh is clearly used to an informal and relaxed atmosphere in his lessons, but, judging by his response to this particular group, he has concluded that their reaction constitutes a challenge to his authority. The group had clearly been noisy at the outset and had not been working productively. The level of noise may have indicated their intention to disrupt the lesson or, at the least to avoid adopting a productive approach. As long as it remained a matter of volume rather than physical disruption, Mr Vangogh may have felt it best to leave things alone. Their involvement in the 'envelope exercise' added a new dimension, however, with overt and openly disruptive behaviour; pulling the envlopes over each other's eyes elicited noisy and fractious responses. These protests naturally attracted the attention of other pupils, rather in the way that a fight or disturbance in the playground always draws the crowds. Such open challenges are likely to spread quickly and Mr Vangogh would have been aware that his reaction to this challenge was being monitored. This would probably take the form of a series of 'flick checks', commonly used by pupils who are deliberately monitoring the teacher's responses following their deviant acts.

Question 2
To some extent their protests may be justified. In their eyes they were only mimicing what the other group had done. What they may not directly be able to perceive is that their particular approach was likely to lead to the involvement of others. Mr Vangogh treated them as if they were well aware of this possibility, and were trying to deny it.

 Mr Vangogh's reaction was quite aggressive: speaking in severe terms, moving forward, invading personal space, pointing, fixing gaze, etc., were all activities designed to place them under considerable pressure and add to his authority. The threat to deprive them of their break was intended to underline his displeasure and emphasise his irritation. From his viewpoint, Mr Vangogh felt it a necessary course of action if he was to neutralise the incident. Their view may have differed as they probably saw this as disproportionate to the crime, particularly in view of the fact that the other group had not drawn his attention and, from their point of view, were equally guilty.

It is essential to his teaching style that Mr Vangogh maintains his reputation for fairness, particularly as he chooses to adopt a fairly informal approach to his classes. His best move now may be to speak to the whole class, including the original group involved in the 'envelope game'. He will need to maintain his relaxed and confident approach, perhaps sitting on the front of the table, call for silence, and address the whole class in a measured and controlled way, fixing his gaze on all the pupils in turn, being careful not to hold the gaze for a period likely to be seen as aggressive or confrontational. Expressing his concern and determination that no behaviour can be tolerated from any pupil that is likely to erode the object of the lesson, he could choose to indicate to the pupils he criticised why he reacted as he did, explaining that he had noticed their intent in developing the game and that they were checking his reaction.

The aggression shown to this particular group need not be shown again, as he has made his point, but he will need to ensure that when he next meets the class he adopts a more salient 'presence' around the classroom, ensuring a more formal approach until the balance of power is fully restored.

Chapter 5

The meaning of pupils' non-verbal signals

Many new and probationary teachers show an unfortunate and almost total lack of awareness of the extent or function of non-verbal pupil behaviours, as we discuss in Chapter 10. In fairness, the signals which predict imminent trouble are subtle and can easily be lost in the mass of non-verbal activity. It is also easy to assume that all deviant behaviour patterns are equal in their challenge to authority. This is not the case. Experienced teachers often 'let things go' and ignore certain potentially disorderly behaviours. They can categorise behaviours in terms of their risk to authority and assess the nature of the challenge being offered – an indispensable skill. They will accept those which offer a low risk. One difficulty in acquiring this skill is that behaviours which indicate potential or actual disruption also occur in other contexts. As a new teacher you may therefore find it difficult to be sure what you are looking at. With the overwhelming mass of events in the classroom, how can you pick out which to react to?

As an indication of the problem in spotting the critical points which require a response, our study of non-verbal teacher and class behaviour, using a computer-based recording system to analyse videotapes, generated about half a million data points per seventy-minute lesson, sampling the teacher and five members of the class every second. If we had been able to sample the remaining twenty or so members of the class, this number would have been correspondingly increased. No human mind could take in and act on all this information, and indeed we usually found that when the teachers looked at tapes of their own lessons, they discovered all sorts of interesting things which they had been unaware of at the time. However, this did not stop them teaching effectively. One of the abilities of experienced and effective teachers is an ability to pick out and read the meaning of the critical non-verbal signals and to ignore the mass of behaviours which have relatively little significance for the overall success and development of the lesson.

There is some evidence that pupils adopt habitual expressions according to their ability, regardless of whether they actually understand what they are being told. In one experiment, low-achieving pupils looked as if they had not understood even simple filmed material, while high achievers acted as if they had comprehended material which was much too complex for their age-group. By behaving in this way, children 'tell' even a teacher who is unfamiliar with them what their academic status is. Additionally, some pupils receive a disproportionate amount of praise from teachers because they are highly rewarding to talk to – using the signals we discuss in Chapter 9 – and teachers, being human, like to talk to people who are responsive. While these are not immediate class management problems, you need to bear in mind the manipulative effects, intentional or otherwise, of pupils' signals.

DISTINGUISHING OPEN AND CLOSED CHALLENGES

As we discussed in the last chapter, it is vitally important for teachers to be able to distinguish the two challenge types – open and closed. The significance of these movement types is not always understood by teachers, and closed or open challenges may be mistaken for mere inattention. As an inexperienced teacher you may *think* you see trouble, but being not quite sure leave it, reluctant to get straight off to an unnecessarily irritable start with the class. Soon enough you will be only too sure that something is wrong. To repeat the distinction made in the last chapter, closed challenges are 'closed' because they will die away if left alone, while open challenges will escalate if left alone. They then become overt threats to the teacher's authority, which the challengers no longer respect.

Open and closed challenges

Deviancy, defined as non-compliance with rules, may take potentially harmless forms; teachers vary in how much attention they pay to these, depending on their own style and the school setting they are working in. Disruption, however, usually requires teacher action as it represents a challenge to authority. We can therefore distinguish *open challenges* which, as their name suggests, 'are intended to enrage the teacher and entertain the whole class' (Macpherson 1983). These have been described by many authors under various names; sometimes a variety of types of open challenge are described. Among the most useful of these descriptions are Macpherson's ('stirring'), Turner's (1983) ('sabotage' and 'refusal') and the activities of Pollard's (1985) primary-school 'gangs'. We have preferred the term 'open challenge', to contrast with *closed challenges*, which are 'not directed to the class as audience and not intended to enrage the teacher' (Macpherson's 'mucking about', Turner's 'withdrawal' and Pollard's 'jokers').

The term 'closed challenge' is intended to imply that these deviancies are conducted within circumscribed limits, are not likely to escalate abruptly (though if completely ignored for long periods they may build up) and do not constitute an immediate challenge to your authority. They represent a self-contained deviation from the task in hand. All you need do is to monitor it and to be seen to be doing so. The children will return to their work often without noticing that you have been aware of what they were doing. Indeed our video study showed that experienced effective teachers noticed incidents of this type when they viewed the videos which they had been unaware of at the time because they were involved with other children. These closed challenges had died away by themselves without teacher and pupils ever having been engaged. If the children do notice that you are aware of them, this will often be sufficient to call them back to their work. Actual intervention may be counter-productive.

You need to distinguish open challenges, which you must tackle, from closed, which you should let alone, if you do not wish to make yourself unpopular with the class by nagging. We give a short checklist here, and explore some of the distinctions – posture, gaze and control checks – in more detail below.

Open challenges   These are usually characterised by:

1 A high level of control checks (Figure 5.1) – the deviants are aware of the risks and are very careful to minimise them by keeping a close eye on the teacher.
2 Variation in gaze direction (the deviants look around the class to locate the teacher and potential allies).
3 Visual involvement of peripheral pupils, who are attracted by the incident and distracted from their work – Figure 5.2.
4 Postural changes to reduce the chances of discovery.
5 Low task involvement.
6 Increased noise level.
7 As the open challenge moves into overt disruption, willingness to argue with the teacher (Figure 5.2) or each other.

In general, open challenges are premeditated, either directed against you as the teacher or against the order you should be maintaining, e.g. kicking another pupil, or taking another pupil's equipment (see the Exercises). They can be distinguished from *overt disruption*, where pupils have decided that you can no longer maintain authority, and that they therefore no longer need to try to conceal what they are doing, and are prepared to confront you directly. We deal with overt confrontations in Chapter 7. Normally, potentially disruptive children will first try you with open challenges; if you do not deal with these satisfactorily they will move to overt disruption. However, particularly difficult children, especially in the middle secondary years, may not go through the initial period of 'testing the water' by open challenges, moving straight to disruption. This is more likely if you do not make a satisfactory initial contact with the class.

Closed challenges   These, on the other hand, are limited to the participants involved (Figures 5.3, 5.4) and normally do not tend to spread. Here the characteristics are:

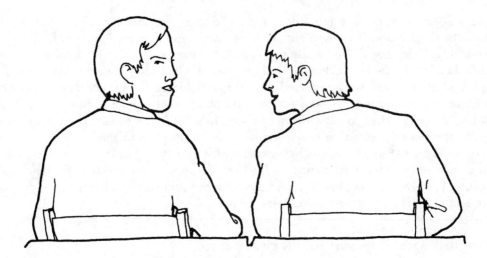

Figure 5.1 A control check or flick check – a rapid glance to assess the whereabouts of the teacher. This suggests the conversation is illicit – compare Figure 4.2 for an ostensibly similar but undisguised conversation

1 Limited gaze direction (only at the other pupil involved), with no attempt to recruit other members of the class (Figure 5.3).
2 Directed conversation (only to the other pupil involved).
3 Relaxed posture (leaning on desk or chair).
4 Few, or no control checks – the children are not trying to keep an eye on the teacher to avoid detection.
5 Rapid head and arm movement – gesturing in relation to their conversation, for example.
6 Increased smiling.
7 Sporadic involvement in the work.

Pupils involved in closed challenges seem almost detached from the direction and pace of the lesson, and their activities are rarely teacher-directed. Their deviancy is also limited in scope and direction, restricted to the other pupils involved – for instance, sharing a joke. These incidents seldom evolve into disruption which carries a high risk to your authority, providing you do not 'stir' them up.

Three subtle differences in pattern between closed challenges and open challenges are worth watching out for: posture, gaze direction and control checks. We will look at each of these in more detail.

Posture

'Posture' refers to the head and body position relative to normal sitting posture. Open challengers show much more variation from normal posture, particularly in head

Figure 5.2 The boy's protest, using the dominant forward baton (Figure 6.12) implies an open challenge to the teacher, which is being monitored by the boy on the next desk. The teacher's hand-on-hips posture, chin down (Figure 6.4), and backward lean indicate resistance, but not escalated to the same level as the boy. Reflecting this, children's responses when shown this picture were mixed: some saw this teacher as 'calm', others as 'angry'

position. Often they will be seen with head low to the desk, sometimes shielded by an arm, bag or the back of the pupil in front. They often sit much lower than usual in their seats. Both these postures conceal their activities from you. Alternatively they may be perched on the edge of the chair, poised to change position in the event of your unwanted attention. Closed challengers usually adopt a more normal seated posture. They are less concerned to conceal what they are doing.

Gaze direction

Gaze direction is more erratic and peer-directed in open challengers. The child appears to be rapidly checking each aspect of his surroundings so his information is as complete as possible before making the next move. On the other hand, plain inattention by closed challengers is often marked by a non-directional blank stare, often directed at

Figure 5.3 Throwing materials, such as this ruler, to friends, is likely to be a 'closed challenge', and a strong reaction may be unwise. Most teachers would not object to materials being passed to a child in the desk in front or behind. Note that they are not checking the whereabouts of the teacher

some inanimate object or scene out of the window! (Figure 5.4). Open challengers look more to their peers. This seems to serve two functions. In addition to seeking approval by holding the gaze of others, they can also recruit a ready assistant if necessary, on whom to off-load or share blame. This reduces your chance of identifying the correct culprit, as both will deny responsibility for the deviant act. Caught in the cross-fire of denial and counterdenial, you have a good chance of retiring confused but wounded.

The control check

The third category, the control check, is more noticeable and easier to associate with an open challenge to teacher authority. Control checks are used to assess the chances of success, and are recognisable as *rapid* and therefore rather furtive glances to check where you are (Figure 5.1). Such 'inappropriate' levels of alertness are important indicators of actual and impending disruption. The control check is shorter in duration than an 'ordinary' look round the classroom, and tends not to follow your movements (this type can also be called a 'flick check'). When spotted, the pupil making the check usually diverts his eyes instantly, avoiding meeting your eye. Often he switches to apparent intent and studious concentration. Only when personally questioned will he make eye-to-eye contact.

Figure 5.4 If she is totally absorbed in the cleanliness of her fingernails (the internal workings of her pen is one among a range of suitable alternatives) she is completely detached from the teacher's lesson plan. This is a closed challenge since she is acting without reference to either the teacher or other members of the class. However, if it becomes apparent to the class that the teacher is prepared to let this pass without comment, she is falling down on her duty to teach, and more open challenges will follow

Sometimes the control check may be longer, if the pupil needs to track your intentions more accurately, but in this case it is still recognisable by the *direct* gaze at you, in conjunction with a rapid gaze-aversion if spotted. This should be taken as a danger signal – why otherwise would the child be so keen to avoid being seen watching? The start of a long control check is also rapid, but is less likely to be seen – if it is, the check will become a short one!

By contrast, when a pupil making a closed challenge looks round, the check is slower both in starting to look at you and in looking away. There is less concern to avoid being detected.

Control checks are most common just before pupils engage in some act of disruption, and again immediately following the act. We can see the way in which control checks operate in this transcript of a disruptive incident sequence involving two pupils, David and Paul, during a secondary Art lesson.

David has returned to his desk after fetching a ruler. As he passes Paul he strikes out with the ruler, hurting him.

Paul:
Moves to avoid ruler.
Makes control check.
Shouts verbal abuse.
Makes control check.

David:
Makes control check.
Stops hitting Paul.
Returns to desk.
Continues with task-directed activity.
Looks provocatively at Paul.

Paul:
Breaks from task directed activity.
Makes control check.
Screws up paper.
Makes control check.
Throws paper at David.
Makes prolonged control check.

David:
Breaks from task.
Makes control check.
Picks up glue spreader.
Makes prolonged control check.
Throws glue spreader at Paul.
Makes final control check.
Resumes task.

Paul:
Makes control check.
Resumes task.

During this sequence a total of ten control checks were made before and after the disruptive event. So well-timed and effective were the checks that none were noticed by the teacher; nor for that matter was the whole incident.

SPOTTING POTENTIAL TROUBLE AS THE CLASS ENTERS

In a previous chapter we saw how dress could be used as a clue to spot potential lively members of the class. Dress should be treated as a closed challenge, if the school rules permit; making a statement this way may prove enough for the pupil concerned. However, the boy in Figure 2.5 (in the Exercises for Chapter 2) indicates an attitude which is far more likely to develop into an open challenge to your authority.

The experienced teacher may choose to ignore this pupil on entry to the classroom, but is more likely to keep an eye on his subsequent behaviour during the lesson. It should be said of course that not all pupils who enter the classroom with seemingly disruptive intent will actually pose a threat to your authority. Many will have arrived at the lesson having been involved in authority struggles elsewhere, and may simply be displaying some signs of agitation. All the more important, then, in this situation to be cautious but at the same time fully aware of the implications displayed in these non-verbal behaviours. If they die away you will have avoided a confrontation; if they do not, you will be able to react promptly.

READING SIGNALS DURING THE LESSON – CLOSED CHALLENGES

During the lesson, both pupil and teacher are continually evaluating performance in terms of authority, status and challenge. The effective teacher formulates an overall picture of relationships in the classroom from the behaviours which can be used to judge how these relationships are developing.

You would no doubt be extremely satisfied during a class discussion with the pupil in Figure 2.9 (Chapter 2 Exercises). This pupil is clearly alert and attentive in his posture and his expression shows puzzled concentration. This represents in many senses the ideal pupil response, although it may be due to fear following an earlier challenge. You might, however, be concerned if it was sustained for a long period. Normally children – or adults for that matter, as can be seen during staff meetings or in-service training – show close concentration only for shortish periods when the topic really interests them, before reverting to a more relaxed attention. If the intent posture is held for a long period it could suggest that the lesson was being pitched at too high a level and that the pupil was getting 'lost', and in due course would give up trying to understand.

It is quite tiring to sustain a high level of postural attention for any length of time. A class will only do so for the whole lesson if the teacher can sustain a riveting performance throughout, and this takes some doing. One example of this from our videotapes was the first Spanish lesson of the term taught by Ms Hola. After an hour's lesson in which the class were on the edge of their seats throughout, she felt she could have done with something stronger than staffroom coffee! Her technique (referred to below in Chapter 6) was to run a lesson primarily concerned with establishing relationships. In this case she conducted the lesson entirely in Spanish, with the class arranged in a horseshoe so she could speak to them individually. The actual lesson content consisted of little more than getting each child to respond in a conversation consisting of 'Hello! My name is . . . What is your name?' This dry content was relieved by intense non-verbal enthusiasm conveyed by intonation, gaze, gesture and head cant (Chapter 7). Her level of effort was clearly justified, in terms of getting the class involved in Spanish and setting up a highly productive relationship for their future work over the school year. She was able to teach in a more relaxed way once her relationship with the class was established. In this case the class's intense concentration reflected intense and pleasurable interest – the accolade for a lively and well-presented lesson. This could be detected by their relaxed faces, rather than the furrowed brow shown in Figure 2.9, smiling or laughing at any interesting or amusing incident. However, Ms Hola's rapid movement round the classroom meant they needed to watch her closely, as they could not tell whom she was going to speak to next. In other words, behind her friendly and supportive approach, which rapidly put her on excellent terms with the class, was the implicit threat of showing up anyone who was inattentive – in Spanish – a fate which befell one or two pupils who risked it.

Normally the class's initial alertness will relax. This can readily be seen among discussion groups of adults, even if they are interested in the topic. This point was brought home forcibly when we attended a discussion group at the end of a conference at the time we were analysing the videotapes of classes. The participants had stayed on specially, in several cases having to rearrange their travel to do so, but within ten minutes they were fiddling with pens, propping their heads on their hands, leafing through papers – all the things we had been watching in apparently disengaged classes.

This relaxation of attention is not necessarily a problem, particularly when the lesson requires pupils to talk to each other or cooperate, and often reflects the children's acceptance of harmonious classroom relationships rather than, as teachers often presume, a comment on the lesson content. Relaxed stances are more common in familiar and comfortable situations, particularly within stable peer associations. Current educational approaches such as active learning seek to make full use of these associations.

However, some postural stances challenge the validity of a lesson, either in terms of its content or its structure, by inappropriate gestures. Frustration may be expressed by tightening the facial skin and lips, scratching the head or leaning on one's hand, holding up the work as if involved in it whilst at the same time staring at you fixedly. Whilst these patterns do not represent an open challenge at this stage, they call for individual attention at some point to avoid disenchantment and rejection later on.

Reading signals during the lesson – signs of danger

There are many situations in all lessons where you can lose the attention of individuals. This can lead to problems later on, both in terms of the amount of work achieved and the level of regard the pupil holds for the value of the lesson, and for you and your right to be there. In looking out for behaviours which indicate detachment from the lesson you must tackle the problem in accordance with the level of the challenge that it actually represents. If you under- or over-react, you risk future problems. Accurate judgement is essential.

Deteriorating concentration may be displayed by signals such as a glazed stare, neutral expression or a head propped on one hand; at this stage these represent only a closed challenge. Most experienced teachers would attempt to draw the pupil back into the lesson, rather than treating it as a serious challenge or even a personal insult. In pupil ratios of 30 or more to one, it is not surprising that individuals become detached on occasions. Figure 5.4, on the other hand, is beginning to show signs of further deterioration in concentration by total, although temporary, detachment from lesson activity. Rapid remedial action is required if this is not to evolve into an open challenge. Leaning back, or resting feet on the chairs would indicate this stage had been reached. This behaviour constitutes an open challenge, even though few words are exchanged, and needs to be dealt with.

Very often these challenges are easily neutralised by subtle moves on the part of the teacher. As we shall see in subsequent chapters, through changes in volume, position-ing, stance and gaze direction, the teacher is able to recall the pupil to the lesson, whilst

Figure 5.5 Yawning is difficult to interpret, as discussed in the text. However, the teacher needs if possible to deal with situations which provoke it because of its contagiousness and ambiguity

giving them the opportunity to retain their dignity and status. In the first two cases it might be sufficient to walk past the pupil and stand close behind him or her but facing away. By facing away your response is only potentially threatening; you could look round and challenge them at any time, but you are not actually doing so. Simply walking past will probably be sufficient to remind the fiddling girl to get on with her work. If you stood over and stared down at a pupil who staring directly at you he might be pressurised into a hostile response; but he cannot challenge your right to stand anywhere you choose in the classroom. To do so is to escalate the dispute; but if he resumes work this is not overtly connected with your move. He does not therefore lose face, because it looks as if he might have been planning to start working again anyhow. Given the choice between clear-cut escalation and unattributably abandoning the challenge, he may well choose to abandon it.

The often voluble yawn illustrated in Figure 5.5 can also represent a significant challenge. Yawning is usefully ambiguous; everyone 'knows' it is an automatic reflex reaction to tiredness or boredom. 'We can't help it' – with the accusing implication that *you* could. In its quietest form, yawning can be taken as a pure physical manifestation of tiredness (what was on the box last night?), a stuffy room or even as an automatic reaction to others having yawned previously. In these cases it can be ignored as a challenge. It can also be a behaviour directed at attracting attention, intended to be heard by all. You should be able to tell if a yawn is aimed at creating a situation and if it might lay the foundations for trouble later on, by the accompanying behaviour. This will have the characteristics of an open challenge – looking to friends, smiling, and a general liveliness out of character with the yawn. General lassitude accompanies a 'closed' yawn.

Situations like these which are not dealt with appropriately can lead to more serious confrontations. It is important to realise that everyone in the classroom is likely to be watching; in Wragg and Wood's (1984) memorable phrase, the first few confrontations of this type in the school year establish 'case law'. They will be taken by some pupils as being situations which require you to respond. Once you respond, pupils can evaluate the effectiveness of your authority. If you completely ignore a behaviour, even a closed challenge, at the start of term, you may be regarded as ineffective. On the other hand if you overreact in a way which is inappropriate to the offence you will be seen as nervous, irrational or vulnerable. The 'knock-on effect' of early open challenges should not be underestimated. So dealing with the signals of pupil detachment requires subtlety and, moreover, sensitivity, both towards the individual and the potential danger of the signal involved in respect of its message to the others in the classroom. Once your relationship with the class is established individual incidents have less significance.

So far we have been looking at behaviours largely confined to the single individual concerned, even though they may convey messages elsewhere, not least to the teacher. However, the inclusion (and in some case intrusion) of other pupils, rapid changes in gaze direction (looking around with the intention of including others), low task involvement and willingness to argue, are all clear signs of an open challenge to your authority. This form of challenge is often directed towards a 'stooge' or 'fall guy', another pupil who may or may not be willingly involved. Both victim and protagonist will claim their innocence loudly and vehemently. If the 'victim' is colluding with his 'attacker', both will gain status if they manage to mislead you. This type of behaviour is fairly easy to observe (though not necessarily to deal with) in a formal teaching environment with pupils sitting in rows. Shouting across the room, pointing, gazing around, all clearly cut across the approved arrangement of the classroom. These behaviours are likely to be less obvious in less formal situations with pupils working in pairs, groups and teams on projects, presentations and in active learning situations.

Surprisingly, open and closed challenge behaviours are still evident in these situations – in some cases even more so – but they can take different and more subtle forms. For example, when pupils are allowed to move freely round the room, in Art or Science practical work, for example, walking around immediately loses its potential value as a challenge. However, the ingenious pupil loses little time in finding an alternative, probably drawing on experience in the less formal world of the primary school.

If group work is handled effectively, it can be immensely productive and rewarding for both the pupil and the teacher. However, when any group is sharing ideas and opinions, intense conversation and reasonably animated behaviour is likely, particularly if ideas need clarification or there is disagreement. There is no reason why pupils working in groups should be any less involved than their adult counterparts, particularly when one considers their complicated and fluid peer group structures (Chapter 1). Noise levels in these situations will inevitably rise. This is bound to cause you anxiety, particularly when you are working in an otherwise monastic environment where noise is taken by your colleagues as an indicator that you do not have effective control.

The situation shown in Figure 5.6 is likely to be a rarity in any lesson, both in frequency and duration! You will probably see this as the ideal working relationship between pupils, with both clearly intent on the exercise, concentrating, focusing and showing all the postural signals one would associate with completing the task. As with

Figure 5.6 The teacher's ideal; concentrated attention to the work, with minimal distraction. The parallel postures indicate they are working separately

all group situations, however, one should expect a fluid movement of behaviour from one state to another. Discussion between pupils working together on an issue should be expected to accompany quiet individual work representing a positive working relationship. We should not forget that individuals will, in these situations, discuss, evaluate, even argue, often creating their own environment, somewhat independent of the overall rules set up by the teacher. Noise levels will rise in the group and it would be sensible to tolerate this, within limits, unless there is some specific reason for requiring individual work or absolute silence.

However, these freer situations provide you with considerable additional control problems. The difficulty is in defining to the class (and yourself) what is an acceptable level of noise and discussion, which is why it sometimes seems better to insist on absolute silence, at the risk of unfriendly relations. As in more formal situations, you should be looking for signs of any move away from a 'closed' approach to the work and interaction ('having a laugh') towards a more open challenge to your authority, using the dynamics of the group situation as a vehicle for such a challenge.

Pupils may become involved in conversations which give the impression that work has ceased and little is being achieved. Provided they are still in 'closed mode', relaxed in posture and restricted in gaze direction, using reciprocal eye contact, there is likely to be little authority challenge here. The effective teacher, with an established class, would probably tolerate this situation, give time for the discussion to terminate naturally, or gently remind the pupils concerned of the need to complete the task. To react to this situation as if it were a challenge would not only be inappropriate but would be likely to create hostility in the pupils concerned, leading to a more serious challenge later on. On the other hand, on first encountering a new class, you should expect them to be more cautious, as you are still an unknown quantity. Prolonged chatting therefore represents a challenge to your authority which you need to deal with gently but without hesitation.

'Open' challenges are often easier to identify in a group activity situation, because they are usually more overt than in the more formal types of lesson. Early clues of intent are often given by the mix and positioning of the group at the start of the lesson. You should be aware of the significance of a clique occupying a table at the rear of the classroom, or of particular individuals placing disproportionate pressure on others to join their group or sit near to them – when their level of interest in the rest of the lesson rarely exceeds or even equals this early animated enthusiasm. Early observation and reaction by the experienced teacher can lessen the chances of challenge and disruption.

It is equally important for you to be alert to inappropriate body language during the lesson itself. If one pupil has moved away from his work and is continually harassing his neighbour, though this behaviour may initially appear to be reasonably self-contained, involving just two individuals, it represents an open challenge. A lack of reciprocal gaze between the two often indicates victim and aggressor. If this situation is ignored by the teacher it would create 'case law' (see above), allowing others to judge the extent of teacher control and to react accordingly.

Despite the knock-on effect, it should be emphasised that it is very rare for all pupils in any particular group to be drawn into an incident. It is rare for more than 10 per cent of the overall group to be willing to involve themselves in open challenges, although there will of course be many interested onlookers whenever a teacher's authority is being tested. Turning around in any situation usually indicates that the individual who is receiving the attention is of reasonably high salience, at least for the moment. After all, turning around is risky activity in the formal classroom, because it is an obvious postural shift inappropriate to most task activities and, most significantly, is easily spotted by the teacher. What is equally significant is the amount of interest shown by other peripheral pupils. The essence of open challenges is their potential to spread beyond those initially involved. If the protagonist can successfully draw others into his sphere of influence, creating a disturbance and breaking task concentration for other pupils, this represents a spreading and serious challenge which needs firm and effective treatment. It is essential that you are careful to apportion any blame to the right pupil or pupils, and not simply assume that all who have stopped work are equally guilty. The ability to pick the correct culprit is what Kounin (1970) calls 'withitness'. If you are not 'withit', you will pick on those who are only reacting to the disturbance. They will resent taking the blame unfairly, while the true perpetrators will ridicule your lack of perceptiveness. This situation is likely to be taken subsequently as 'case law', so you must get it right.

SUMMARY

Open challenges, which are a serious threat to teacher authority and must be dealt with, need to be distinguished from closed challenges, which will die away by themselves if left alone. Responding to a closed challenge may be counter-productive, leading it to escalate. Open and closed challenges can be distinguished by a range of non-verbal clues: vigilant 'control checks' to see whether the teacher is aware of the challenge, and looking around to locate and involve other pupils are characteristic of open challenges. Vigilance is necessary to spot the original offender; if you can do this correctly it shows the class you are 'withit'. Closed challenges are more relaxed and less furtive. Pupils normally relax over the course of a lesson, and what appear to be mild closed challenges may merely reflect this relaxation. Open challenges may be marked by signals indicating clear detachment from the lesson, such as inappropriate dress or meeting the gaze of the teacher defiantly, either at the start of the lesson or during it. Informal or 'open' classrooms can lead to patterns which are less easily recognised as challenges than their counterparts in the formal classroom. Inappropriate or excessively friendly behaviour is an example.

The training materials are related to the important task of distinguishing the cues which indicate how serious a challenge is.

TRAINING MATERIALS

Most people have a well-defined sense of fairness. From toddlers to pensioners we can always be sure of hearing tragic tales of how unfair the world is! Surprisingly, perhaps, the notion of 'fairness' is also central to successful classroom control.

Research has shown that many deviant pupils accept that there is some danger in their actions and that, to a greater or lesser extent 'it's a fair cop' if they are caught. There is no greater threat to classroom control, however, than a class that believes that the teacher is unfair, either in her judgement as to which individuals were responsible, or in the nature of her punishments, particularly when they do not appear to fit the crime.

It is useful, then, to be able to recognise a genuine challenge to authority (those classified as 'open challenges and likely to continue if they remain unchecked) and 'closed challenges' (those of a more parochial nature, not aimed at or intending to erode teacher authority and status).

The first set of pictorial exercises are intended to evoke thought and discussion as to what visual clues may allow you to distinguish how serious a challenge different behaviours represent.

Pictorial Exercise – 'Who, me?'

Question 1   Imagine that the four scenes shown in Figures 5.7–5.10 took place in your lesson. Rank them in order of their perceived challenge to your authority.

For each, say also whether you would consider this an open challenge to your authority. What is the evidence for your view and what are the most significant non-verbal clues?

Question 2   Look also at the scene depicted in Figure 5.11, which was taken from a lesson that later proved to be very difficult for the teacher concerned. This group of individuals eventually provided a direct challenge to her authority.

There are three clear indicators of open challenge here, can you identify them? Is there any evidence that this outburst may spread to others?

Figure 5.7

Figure 5.8

Figure 5.9

Figure 5.10

Figure 5.11

Descriptive Exercise –'Paul'

Every class has a potential "Paul"; a pupil who always seems on the edge of the lesson, not wholly involved, but not always actively disruptive. The three situations below chart Paul's contribution and invite you to formulate an approach of your own.

Situation 1
Paul has not taken an active part in your lesson; he has leant on his elbow throughout your introduction and gazed out of the window. He has not spoken to anyone else, but when you ask the class to begin, he leans back on his chair discussing with those behind what it is that they have been asked to do.

Question What would be your reaction, and how would you approach Paul?

Situation 2
Paul is now sitting sideways on his chair and leaning against the wall. He has opened his book, but has not written anything, as others have been doing for some time. You move to Paul to speak to him again and he averts his eyes, playing with the buckle on his bag as you are talking.

Question What are his actions saying, and how could you respond?

Situation 3
Paul has now involved another pupil in his disaffection. They have been generally 'messing about' for some minutes, but their activities have remained confined to themselves. You ask Paul to move, indicating that he should sit nearer to you. He replies 'What for?', staring at you directly and leaning back on his chair as he does so. His friend immediately returns to work.

Question What does Paul's reaction tell you about:

1 His attitude to the situation?
2 The steps you would need to take to avoid further deterioration of the situation?

How would you emphasise your determination to correct the situation?

Remember, there may not be a single 'perfect' reaction to the situations outlined above, but exploring the possibilities may help in developing future strategies. Consider Paul's situation as you move through the remaining chapters; hopefully further strategies will suggest themselves by the time you reach the end of the book.

TRAINING MATERIALS – ANSWERS TO EXERCISES

Figure 5.7   Out of the four incidents illustrated we ranked this as number two. Any pupil who physically interferes with another during a lesson is always likely to be somewhat detached from the legitimate course of the lesson. When such interference is accompanied by an open backward lean and the victim is a pupil who has been trying to work, then action must be taken. At this stage, of course, the incident may not involve others, or even have attracted their attention: all the more important to deal with it before it becomes a source of entertainment for all. Another of our videotapes showed a similar incident in a first lesson where the aggressor leaned over and actually bit the victim's shoulder! Again the victim had been totally involved in his work. His shout of protest brought the teacher across, and this prompt reaction was sufficient. In fact the teacher misidentified who had been shouting, but as his approach was jovial and he rapidly moved on to a friendly discussion, no long-term offence was caused.

Figure 5.8   Ranked four on our list of nasties; shouting across to friends constitutes an open challenge, though the same posture displayed silently, for instance to request a pencil or rubber, might not be (compare Figure 5.3 for a closed challenge). The undisguised posture suggests he expects little challenge from the teacher and little challenge is what he should receive, at least to begin with. Your mere presence in close proximity should be enough to silence this character and return him to the task at hand.

Figure 5.9   Ranked one on our list, this is a potentially serious situation. It may well be that he has been asked to give out the books, in which case, quite apart from the irreverent treatment that they are receiving (which is likely to cause protests from the recipient), he is making an open show of his deviance which is quite deliberately designed to involve others in the room. Additional evidence to confirm your concern could be found in his dress. If he is still wearing his coat, when it is clear that the other pupils are not, this shows, at the very least, his contempt for the system, if not for the rules laid down by the teacher. Firm action needs to be taken here. For a start, he should not have been allowed to give out the books until he had taken off his coat. The rule that books are carried, not thrown, would need enforcing, whether he is distributing books for the teachers or returning one to a friend.

Figure 5.10   Ranked three on our list. The hunched posture indicates an open challenge, with the use of arm and bag as conscious protection against detection of their conversation (compare Figure 4.2). The grin from the boy behind shows the interaction set is beginning to spread, but it is still localised, as the next pair behind are still busy with their work. The conversation needs dealing with at this stage. If left it would become more overt as the two at the front turn round to talk to their friend behind, and perhaps more are drawn in. However, a mild corrective move, such as moving close to the group, should be sufficient.

Figure 5.11   This represents a potentially volatile situation, as all the hallmarks of an open challenge are present. Clear aggressive gestures combine an apparent accusation with a measure of 'what are you going to do about it?' expectancy. The involvement of peripheral pupils – turning around, smiling etc. – indicates the potential for the situation to spread. If left unchecked, this situation could escalate and involve a high proportion of the class. As so many pupils are party to the situation this is a direct challenge to the teacher. Failure to act appropriately will erode all authority. Removal and resiting of the offending pupil from the group would be an immediate solution – but which pupil, the accused or the accuser? This picture was taken from a lesson that significantly deteriorated from this point on, largely because the accused (boy front right) was removed! The massive sense of injustice felt by the boy concerned and his followers was carried into several subsequent lessons with the teacher involved, an indication that you need to observe all features of pupil interaction.

Descriptive Exercise – 'Paul'

Situation 1
You would be forgiven for being irritated in the extreme, but it is clear from Paul's initial behaviour that this may not be a deliberate act. Gazing out of the window is a localised behaviour and not a open challenge to your authority, as it involves no one else. As for not listening to instructions, annoying though it is, it is common both within and outside of the classroom and should not be taken personally; after all, have you never been in a meeting where you lost your place on the agenda? Of greater concern is the leaning back. If it is brief and it is clear from their neutral faces and direction of gaze that he is genuinely asking for information, he can be left; if not, particularly if he is smiling or leaning in an ostentatious way, it may be worth keeping a close eye on him.

Situation 2
Paul's disaffection is growing, for whatever reason, and it is clear by now that action must be taken if you are to rescue the situation. Sitting sideways on the chair gives Paul visual access to a larger proportion of the class and leaning against the wall is a relaxed signal demonstrating to all that he is not intending to work. Moving towards Paul as you speak to him is important, as you are seen to invade on his personal space. Averting his eyes as you talk to him shows a reluctance to actually challenge your authority; this response is both defensive and submissive. Firmness is essential here and is unlikely to be resisted. You should use your authority to redirect him, both physically and intellectually.

Situation 3
Paul is certainly intending to test your authority, but he will not be fully sure of his ground as the fact that his accomplice has returned to work has left him somewhat isolated. The fixed stare is undoubtedly aggressive and is reinforced by leaning back, indicating that he may be relaxed in making this challenge and feels in control. Moving him is correct as most pupils see it as a legitimate use of teacher authority. However, his challenging question has caused a delay, during which time other class members will be drawn to the confrontation.

The quick return to work by Paul's accomplice may give a clue to your next move. Clearly this other pupil is not prepared to challenge you directly and if you ask him to move he is more likely to do so without protest. Having established your authority over this pupil in front of the class you are in a stronger position to move Paul. You should refuse to enter a discussion as to 'why' and point out the consequences of further refusal to move. It may be worth adding that he may find himself working closer to you on a regular basis and for some considerable time to come. Picking up his book, walking away and placing it on the designated table may be effective. Pupils see teachers as having the authority to move and collect items of school equipment without having to ask permission. To object to your doing so would be a further escalation of his challenge, which he may not be willing to risk.

Chapter 6

Getting attention

FACING THE MULTITUDE

You may need to get attention in a number of situations; in the playground or corridors, or when starting a lesson. The techniques for confidently getting attention are the same in all these situations, and they apply to other members of staff such as playground supervisors as well as teachers.

In a lesson, your first task is to get the class to pay attention to what you are about to say. Lessons fall into segments, and if the lesson is to fit the plan you have produced, you need to control the transition from one segment to another. This need arises at the start of the lesson whether the children are already in their working positions when you join them, or whether they are lined up outside and need to quieten down before they can be brought into the classroom. It arises again whenever you need to explain the organisation of the next part of the work, get the class to listen to the next part of the lesson theme, set homework, or to get the children to stop what they are doing and clear up.

These transitions between segments are purely administrative and contribute nothing to the children's learning – on the contrary, they can offer considerable possibilities for delay, and worse, if the children suspect you are not in command of the situation. Organising groups in corridors, in the playground or dining room, or in assembly puts the same demands on whoever is required to do it.

As a teacher you also need their attention to get across the excitement of what you are teaching them, your pleasure in their progress and your interest in them as persons. Control has positive value as well as its neutral or negative aspects.

Communicating relaxed control demands considerable subtlety in non-verbal communication, both in posture and timing. Too much verbal communication can indeed be counter-productive – the more you nag at children, the less likely you are to be taken seriously. Your manner must convey that you expect the attention of the class, and that having got it, you can act decisively to carry out the teaching objective which was your aim when calling for attention in the first place.

Mark my words

One characteristic of teachers' talk is their use of *markers*; signals to draw the class's attention to the actual message which follows (Sinclair and Coulthard 1975). Markers convey no information themselves, but they reassert your control over the classroom and save time by ensuring messages do not need to be repeated. If the class are already mostly attending to you, the postures we describe below serve to mark the importance of what you are saying. If the class are talking, usually some sort of sound marker will be necessary to draw their attention; in most cases a verbal instruction to stop and listen will be sufficient – '2OW, listen please!'. In noisy situations, such as class oral work in foreign languages, home economics, science and crafts, some more distinctive signal, such as banging a board-rubber or rolling-pin on a table, may be necessary, and where there are safety implications instant attention will have to be enforced as a rule. (We will come on to enforcement in Chapters 8 and 9). Incidentally, the fact that a sharp rap on the desk serves perfectly well as a marker confirms the point we made above, that markers convey only very limited information and do not really need to be dignified by words.

Immediately you call for attention, you will run into reactions from the class which, if you are uncertain, are likely to put you off your stride. The class may simply not attend; they may continue to chat to their friends, wander around, or worse. In this case you have a potential problem; we will deal with the tactics to cope with this in Chapter 8. With luck, on a first encounter, the children will stop what they are doing, and attend to you closely: and this may immediately put you into a position you find difficult. Being stared at by a large number of people can be an unfamiliar and threatening situation. To understand why this is, we need to consider your previous experience of being looked at, as this is the basis on which you respond. If you are unfamiliar with talking to groups, you will interpret the children's response in terms of your previous conversational experience.

By adulthood, most people have developed high levels of skill in informal social situations, such as talk between friends. In normal social conversation people do not stare at each other intensely for long periods; in fact listener and speaker in conversation look at each other only briefly. The speaker glances occasionally at the listener to check he is still attending: while the listener watches the speaker for most of the time, he tends to avert his gaze quite rapidly when she looks at him (Ellis and Beattie 1986). We are all highly sensitive to variations in this pattern, which can be measured in milliseconds, though we are usually quite unconscious of them. Most important in the present context is how we interpret an extension of the periods of mutual gaze, due to the listener not looking away when the speaker looks at him. This indicates strong interest by the listener, though normally the effect is very subtle, the mutual gaze being just a fraction longer than usual. A steady stare normally indicates strong emotion, either passionate attachment or anger (Morris 1977). Problems arise when the conversational pattern changes to that of a many-to-one situation, yet you continue to use the interpretations you are used to.

When a single speaker is talking to a group, the normal balance of gaze of a one-to-one conversation is disrupted. You have to distribute your attention and your gaze across the whole class, so you will only look at each child occasionally. At this point, following the usual rules of mutual gaze, he will probably look away. By then, however, you may well have gone on to the next child; you will find this one is still looking at you, because, so far, you have not been looking at her. The pattern will repeat itself as you look round the class. If you now look back to the first child, you will find him looking at you again because, of course, you have not been looking at him for some time. If you find the class gazing fixedly at you, you will probably not use Morris's first interpretation of what is happening: few classes fall in love with their teacher at first sight! If you are already slightly anxious, you are likely to interpret this characteristic level of looking by a group as threatening, especially as the facial expressions of concentration and that of mild anger are identical. (In both cases the mouth is neutral and gaze is direct, with brows drawn slightly down and together at the inner corners.) If you then behave in an uncertain way, your inability to cope will immediately become obvious because the whole class is watching you.

The response you display to the children must not be one of anxiety; they must see relaxation or a very mild level of threat, indicating that you expect and have a right to their attention. It is worth saying right away that the threat must be so mild that the children do not consciously perceive it as threat, but see you as 'able to keep order'; extreme non-verbal threat (Chapter 7) may be as counter-productive as verbal nagging.

If you are uncertain, you inevitably tend to avoid the gaze of the class, by looking down at the register or your lesson notes, for instance (Figure 6.1), or later, when you have started the lesson, at what you have written on the board. It is important to avoid this as far as possible, despite the strong temptation to look at your only friend in the room – something which will not stare back. Even more undesirable is the pattern sometimes seen in student teachers on teaching practice, of totally avoiding the gaze of the class by looking in an unfocused way into the middle distance. Subordinates avert their gaze; dominants do not.

Failure to look at someone when you are talking to them is also interpreted as betraying a lack of interest in them. You are thus doubly damned. By looking away too much you appear both weak-willed and cold – not a good start for gaining the respect and approval of the class. The second pattern – the unfocused gaze – seldom persists for long in either probationers or experienced teachers; complete lack of communication soon leads to complete lack of control and a rapid exit from the profession.

Looking confident

Dominant individuals appear relaxed, and beginning teachers are often urged to behave casually – just to do what they would normally if they were not standing in front of a

Figure 6.1 Looking down – one form of gaze aversion from the class. Many children saw this teacher as 'boring' or 'serious'

class. The problem with this is that very few of us are *aware* of what we do normally, when we are not thinking about what we are doing. As soon as we start thinking about what we are doing, our behaviour is liable to change simply because we have started thinking about it!

Three obviously casual postures are standing with hands in the pockets and leaning or sitting on furniture; these are suited to quiet classes where you are not likely to meet an immediate challenge. For livelier classes, one of the mildly threatening postures described later would be a better choice.

One great advantage of the hands-in-pockets posture is that it prevents your hands betraying your nervousness by fumbling or fiddling – provided you do not jingle your loose change. A loose jacket or something similar is best for a casual posture; tight trouser or jeans pockets give a rather strait-jacketed and tense effect. It should be possible to abandon the jacket after one or two sessions. Fumbling and self-grooming are among a whole range of nervous tics of which teachers are often blissfully unaware while their classes are only too aware – as is often clearly demonstrated in end-of-term skits. You should try to get your mannerisms – with the aid of a well-disposed colleague if you cannot spot them yourself – before they get you.

Sitting on a desk similarly avoids the risk of pacing about, rocking from side-to-side or advancing and retreating incessantly from the class which you may indulge in if you are standing up. These are *intention movements* of escape from the unpleasant situation you find yourself in: the unconscious desire to get away is suppressed, but not soon enough. They can be extremely distracting. Most recently qualified teachers will be familiar with the lecturer who paces to and fro like a caged wolf at the zoo; usually this is about the only memorable feature of his lectures. It is obviously inappropriate for you to give the impression that you are desperate to get out of the door if only you could find it, but these movements can be very difficult to control; in general we are less conscious of our feet than of our facial expression or even our hands. Sitting down can reduce this *leakage* of uncertainty (you may swing your feet, but this is not quite so obvious). It is still important to avoid wriggling around uncomfortably, or sitting tensely with arms pressed into the sides. You should sit firmly on the desk and avoid intention movements of getting up, which are just as distracting as pacing around. One student teacher recorded on our videotapes during her first lesson gave an excellent impression of a cat sitting on a hot tin roof, bouncing off her desk every minute or so. She was unaware of what she was doing because of her nervousness, but the class loved it. She was just leaning against the desk, which makes it much easier to make these movements unintentionally. When the problem was pointed out to her, she was able to avoid it in subsequent lessons.

Except in special circumstances (for instance, if the class is sitting round in a circle informally) you should always be at a higher level. Height is an indicator of dominance. (This, incidentally, is another reason for the 'caged-wolf' behaviour; the threatening effect of being stared at by a whole class is increased if they are all looking down at the lecturer, as happens in most conventional banked lecture theatres.) The people who put pulpits in churches knew what they were doing; it is much easier to lecture in a theatre with even a slight dais, of the type found in turn-of-the-century classrooms.

If you are sitting at the same level as the class you will also be unable to see them all, as the children in front will block your view of those behind. When you are sitting on a desk or other surface, if possible you should have a chair or stool to rest your feet on. This tends to encourage a forward-leaning posture, whereas without a footrest the posture you need to adopt for balance is upright, or leaning slightly back.

Leaning forward towards the person you are speaking to communicates greater involvement, whatever you are talking about – you will appear more friendly, more interested in your subject, or more forcefully in control. The same effect can be achieved when standing up by a forward lean on the table, provided you make sure to meet the children's gaze (compare Figure 6.1). If you are an uncertain beginning teacher, the table also provides a barrier between yourself and the class which gives useful psychological security. If this security makes you more forthcoming, its beneficial effects will usually outweigh the extra distance it imposes between you and your class, and it should soon be possible to come out from behind the desk.

Here comes trouble

When you have to deal with a more recalcitrant class, signals such as leaning on the table and barrier signals should take rather different forms. The asymmetric lean on the table, often with one hand on the hip, is a classic teacher posture (Figure 6.2). It neatly combines relaxed indifference (the asymmetric posture and lean) with threat (the hand on hip). Standing with both hands on the hips is more directly threatening, though children usually perceive it as 'irritable' or 'impatient'. The hands on hips make

Figure 6.2 The combined hand-on-hip and sideways lean signals both threat and indifference. The ambivalent posture produced a variety of responses from children, but many saw this teacher as 'calm'

Figure 6.3 Chin-up, or 'plus face'. The raised chin, direct stare and slightly raised brows are a signal of dominance widely used among young children, though the face is less often seen among older children and adults. Though this posture is often described as 'looking down your nose at somebody', its significance as a signal of dominance is not widely known

Figure 6.4 Chin-down threat. This is a less dominant position than the head-up 'plus face' (Figure 6.3); it would become a submissive face if the gaze were dropped as well. It communicates defiance rather than dominance.

you look bulkier (especially if you are wearing fairly loose clothing, which fills in the gaps). The posture also arches the back and pulls the head back (try it). This tends to bring the chin forward and up, which is a signal of dominance employed from early childhood (hence the expressions 'to look down your nose at' or 'look down on' another person (Figure 6.3). Its opposite is the chin-down, gaze-averting posture of submission (Figure 6.4).

Be warned that looking down at a book or papers on your desk superficially resembles the chin-down posture. This does not matter if it occurs only briefly, but if anxiety makes you avert your gaze, as mentioned above, the class is likely to take advantage. If possible, you should avoid the intermediate pattern, with chin down but looking at the class. This gives a 'cornered' impression; the posture is submissive, but continuing to meet the gaze of the opponents conveys defiance. You probably do not much more want to look like a cornered rat than a defeated one.

The symmetrical hands-on-hips posture, though effective when quietening a noisy class, gives rather too much of a hectoring impression if used excessively; folding the arms gives the same impression of refusing to budge, but is less threatening because the arms now form a barrier in front of the body. Many people find the arms fold a comfortable resting position, and it makes a useful standby. It is the most assertive of a range of *body cross* positions, most of which give an impression of uncertainty and should be avoided if possible. However, it is both impossible and unnecessary to avoid them completely – teaching involves constant stress, from the need to make on-the-spot decisions, and experienced teachers who have good relationships with and control over their classes frequently show the body cross and other stress patterns described below. As an inexperienced teacher, you should only worry if these patterns are major elements in your behaviour, especially when you are trying to get the attention of the class.

Figure 6.5   Self-hold body cross, a barrier signal with elements of tension. There are a variety of self-holding postures, all of which serve a self-reassuring function; they are shown by many teachers, including some who have very effective relationships with their classes. Given that, like the arms-fold, they allow the teacher to reduce her stress level, and that children are not very sensitive to their meaning, teachers should not feel under particular pressure to eliminate them

Signs of stress

Morris (1977) has argued that self-touching is a powerful source of reassurance, and most people touch themselves in stressful situations, though they may not be conscious of doing so. When you were little you clung to your parents at times of trouble; as an adult you may be forced to cling to yourself, providing the reassuring touch which would be provided by a friend if one were available. The self-hold arm-cross (Figure 6.5) and similar postures provide this reassurance. Very often you need to have a piece of chalk, a worksheet or a pen at the ready; usually these are held in a mild or ambivalent form of body cross, but you should try to avoid slipping into what

Robertson (1989) has nicely called the 'waiter posture', clutching the textbook or whatever desperately to your bosom as a shield against whatever the class may throw at you. All these arm positions give a closed-in, withdrawn impression.

Figure 6.6 Clothes groom (left) and head groom (right). The head groom is a ritualisation of an originally threatening posture, and is seen as indicating 'gets upset' by many children. Most teachers groom at moments of stress; this is a behaviour pattern which may cause no trouble unless it becomes excessive

Another frequent response to a need for reassurance is to make grooming movements to clothes or head (Figures 6.6, 6.7), or to fumble with something. Alternatively you may bring a hand to cover or massage the face (Figure 6.8) – this also serves to create a barrier between the mouth or face and the audience, like a miniature version of the body cross. While this is associated with uncertainty in general, it is particularly characteristic of lying or deceitfulness – not quite the impression you want to create about your subject-matter! If these movements are repeated over any length of time they can become extremely distracting to the class. Very often you yourself are totally unaware of them. As they can be a fruitful source of material to the impressionist who lurks in many classes, it is worth checking with friends or colleagues if they are conspicuous, and trying to avoid showing them if they are. The same applies to a range of facial expressions of stress , such as pressing or licking your lips (Figure 6.9), pulling them in or back (Figure 6.10), or biting them (Figure 6.11). One of the effects of anxiety

Figure 6.7 Taken from a videotape of the first lesson of a teacher who went on to have severe discipline problems. In one movement she combines a body cross and fumbling with her clothes, both indications of uncertainty

is to dry up the flow of saliva, and these movements are an unconscious reaction to the dry-mouthed feeling which results. If detected by the class, they convey uncertainty.

Again, as an inexperienced teacher, you should not get too anxious about ever showing these expressions of stress. They are commonly shown by effective teachers, especially when they know they are approaching a confrontation – for instance, criticising the standard of the class's homework. However, as soon as such teachers move to get the class's attention, the stress signals disappear. As a result, most of their classes only see these teachers looking confident; few were looking at them before they called for attention, when they were betraying momentary anxiety. Experienced teachers also often show a stress reaction, frequently a hair groom (Figure 6.6) after a crisis has been resolved. As the teacher moves away, after the recalcitrant child has been put firmly in his place, she runs her hand through her hair. Again, this is likely to go unnoticed, as by then the class has settled once more to its work. This behaviour is not confined to classrooms; motorists do the same after a near miss, for instance. Teaching is a stressful business, and the new teacher cannot hope to avoid showing

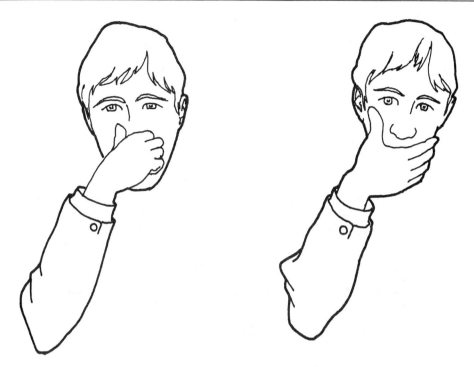

Figure 6.8 Hand to nose (left) and hand to mouth (right). The hand to mouth posture is often used by teachers as a ritual sign of uncertainty, for instance when they are listening to a child trying to answer a difficult question, to indicate to the child that the problem really is difficult. Hand to nose, a more disguised sign of uncertainty, is less common

stress completely; if you know what to look for in your apparently ice-cool colleagues, you may be reassured by seeing they have their hidden problems too.

What Katy did next

We have not spent a lot of time on how to get the attention of the class because it should not be a major section of the lesson in terms of time; rather the reverse! Dominant and relaxed individuals are decisive; having got the attention of the class, you should then move *rapidly* on to whatever was your aim in calling for attention (Figure 6.12). Non-verbal signals, like words, are only promises of action; having promised, you must act. If you dawdle, the initial attention will be dissipated very soon. It may be desirable to start on the main activity once you have got the attention of most members of the group, rather than nagging the last few to attend. It is critical to judge correctly, if the last few are challenging you openly, whether they have the support of the rest of the group, as we discussed in Chapter 4. If they do not, you can proceed and they should become involved as the purpose of the activity becomes clear and they will be under some pressure to conform with the cooperative majority. If they fail to do so,

Figure 6.9   Lick lips (left) is a result of a physiological response to stress; under stress, saliva production is reduced, and the mouth feels dry. The tongue may also be protruded, and held in this position, at moments of concentration (a pattern which can sometimes be seen in young children or sportsmen who are cencentrating); it has been shown that people tend to avoid distracting someone who is tongue-protruding. Press lips (right) is a mild version of one of the characteristic mouth expressions of anger. Many children described this teacher as 'boring'

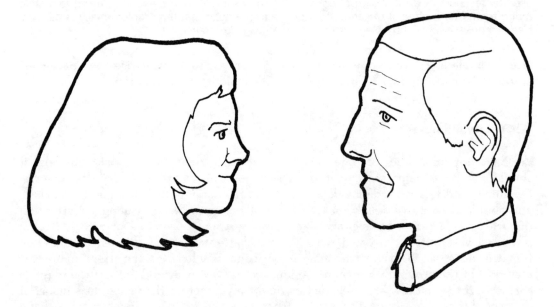

Figure 6.10   Lips in (left), another variant of the lip bite; tight mouth (right), a mild type of fear mouth; the retracted corners of the mouth are shown in a more extreme form in real fear

Figure 6.11 Lip bite, another anxiety signal. These signals normally go unnoticed by the teacher who is producing them, or the class, and children had difficulty in interpreting them; but they may surprise and shock a teacher who sees herself recorded on video

they can be tackled individually once the main group is occupied, when they should be less likely to play to the gallery. Arguing it out with the last few may serve solely to create problems by distracting the law-abiding. However, if they have the attention of the rest of the class, you will need to tackle it as a serious confrontation (Chapter 8).

Your tasks when you call for the attention of the class on the first occasion you meet them will probably include calling the register, distributing books, telling the class the rules which will apply in the classroom and what they will be doing during the year. Only the last of these is strictly educational, and it is desirable to move on with reasonable rapidity to work related to the subject. Thus it is preferable to go through the register quickly and to connect names and faces while going round the class later on when the children are working; occasionally, as in oral work in languages, it may be possible to get children to give their names during the course of the work. Similarly, it may be possible to save time by giving books out in a batch for each row (and collecting them in the same way) so that the children have less time to engage in conversation with their neighbours. Once the class is known to be orderly, pupils can assist with such tasks to speed things up.

Too long a catalogue of rules at the start gives the impression that you are expecting trouble. It may even put ideas into their heads as to how they can cause annoyance.

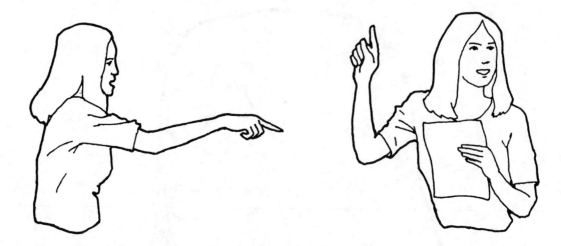

Figure 6.12   Forward baton (left); it differs from pointing, as the hand is moved forcefully, and the finger points towards the child being spoken to, not an object (see also Figures 4.3 and 7.7). Most children saw this teacher as 'strict'. Upward baton (right), also a dominant signal, usually used to enforce attention to what is being said. Children were divided in their understanding of this, but tended to positive reactions, such as 'friendly' and 'helpful'

Experienced teachers usually deal with the rules for each situation, such as the presentation of written work and when homework is to be handed in, as it arises during the context of the lesson. In most subjects, the children already have a fair idea of how the work is to be done, and you can often transmit your expectations positively by praising early examples of satisfactory work, for instance as you go round the classroom (Chapter 9).

In some practical subjects, such as Science, children will need to master a considerable number of rules when they encounter the subject for the first time, and these will have to be taught as for other subject-matter, using the methods for interesting and involving the class described in Chapter 7. Science, Craft and Physical Education teachers have no special legal protection in view of the rather more hazardous nature of their lessons, and are under the same obligation as other teachers to ensure that children are protected against foreseeable hazards while under their care (Partington 1984). Your legal obligation not to allow children to put themselves into danger places a special responsibility on you in these subjects, but you have to rely on your authority and a convincing manner to make sure that the children believe the dangers they describe are real. In view of children's cheerful indifference to danger, you cannot rely on them making the judgement an adult would in the same circumstances. They will probably be convinced mainly by your credibility, though you may need some demonstrations or blood-curdling examples of what happens when safety precautions are neglected to convince the class that you are not crying wolf.

The purpose of the techniques in this chapter is merely to ensure that you can hold the children's attention so that you are in a position to start teaching or whatever other activity you are engaged in. If you are to sustain this attention for the duration of a lesson, let alone for a whole year, you must communicate to them that what you have to teach is interesting and worth learning (Chapter 7) and that you are interested in and care about them (Chapters 7 and 9).

SUMMARY

Attention-getting skills are particularly important in maintaining control and avoiding waste of time at the start of lessons and when moving from one section of the lesson to another. Clear marker signals are needed to attract attention; the class then should see relaxed or extremely mild threat signals, such as sitting or leaning on a table. These examples signal dominance through superior height. Stress signals such as self-holding, avoiding looking at the class and intention movements of escape will be detected, as the class will be paying close attention, particularly in the first lessons of the year, when the teacher–class relationship is being established.

Having gained attention, it is then necessary to show you can act decisively; administrative tasks should be dealt with rapidly and efficiently.

It is useful to watch senior staff getting attention with large groups, such as in assembly, where the problems are intensified. The training materials consider which attention-getting signals are effective.

TRAINING MATERIALS

If you were to ask the average experienced teacher to describe the most threatening teacher/pupil situation they can imagine, most would reply with accord – taking Assembly! This is not because they are likely to be lost for words (they will probably have spent weeks preparing it), nor is it likely to reflect any particular religious objection, but with the numbers involved and the uncertainty of the situation it is likely to bring back painful memories of their early days in teaching when getting attention was so essential and, on occasions, so problematic.

It is, in fact, a useful source of technique to watch experienced teachers take an Assembly or large meeting, because the skills they use have been carefully selected and successfully applied over the years for the purposes of getting attention.

Pictorial Exercise – 'Now hear this'

This first exercise has as much to to with the Assembly scenario as the lesson situation.

Question 1   Examine the four signals illustrated in Figures 6.13 and 6.14.

If these were displayed in a lesson situation, which do you think would be most successful in helping to ensure the class's attention? What messages are being transmitted in each?

Would your opinions differ if these were displayed in front of a large group as opposed to a class-sized group? What differences would you expect to see between these situations?

Question. 2   What are your feelings when faced with the picture in Figure 6.15? Do you feel uneasy in any way? If so, why?

Do all the individuals shown here have the same effect on you? Are some sending a different message, and can you identify what that might be?

Figure 6.13

Figure 6.14

Figure 6.15

Descriptive Exercise – 'An Inspector calls'

There are always a range of factors facing you whenever you meet your next class, and some of these can affect the speed and efficiency with which you are able to gain their attention. In the following example, Andy, a Middle School teacher of three years' experience, is about to be observed by a visiting Inspector as he takes a year 7 Drama lesson. To make matters worse, Andy has only been told of this an hour before, at the same time in fact that the Head declared his own intention to be present!

Andy had spent his break, or what there was of it, double-checking his preparation for the lesson. He generally enjoyed teaching Drama, although not a specialist, and was not over-concerned with the noise generated or the obvious excitement displayed by some of the class.

Andy arrived late, having returned to the staffroom to retrieve the preparation he had so lovingly produced. The class had already entered, removed their outdoor shoes as per the usual routine and were sliding across the floor of the hall — the caretaker's pride and joy! The Inspector and the Head were there too.

Andy held his file in his left hand, looked around the hall at the well-dispersed class, and called for quiet in a moderate tone. Acutely aware of time, or the lack of it, owing to his lateness, he glanced several times at his watch. He called again asking the class to 'sit on the floor in front of him'.

The majority responded, many demonstrating the technique of precision sliding as they arrived expertly at his feet, blissfully unaware of the presence of the VIPs. Some were engrossed in other activities, however, and were called again, this time with considerable volume, accompanied by an angry frown and a specific stare.

Eventually the class gathered at Andy's feet and he began the lesson introduction. Nearly ten minutes had passed since the lesson bell. Andy explained the lesson format to the pupils, even mentioning the skills and concepts involved, which passed several feet over their heads. His academic performance completed, Andy attempted to divide the class into mixed-sex groups, but before he could complete his directions some of the class had drifted away again and were practising stocking pirouettes.

Acutely aware of being observed, Andy moved from his usual pattern of behaviour. He threw his file on the floor, making a loud cracking noise, shouted 'enough!', pointed to the floor immediately in front of him and said in a quiet but pronounced tone, 'You will all come and sit here now and in silence, or Drama will be a thing of the past.' They returned in silence and Andy stood, head up and gazed momentarily at each child in turn without a word being exchanged on either part.

Question 1. Andy was clearly concerned by the whole situation. In what ways do you feel that this may have leaked to the pupils?

Question 2 In your opinion, do you feel that the class were out of control or was there a conflict in style brought about by the unusual situation?

Question 3 The turning point seemed to be when, in exasperation, the file was thrown to the floor. Why, in this situation, was this so effective and how was it reinforced?

Question 4 If you were the Inspector, how would you have commented on the first fifteen minutes of Andy's lesson?

TRAINING MATERIALS – ANSWERS TO EXERCISES

Figure 6.13 'Waiter' posture (left). Join hands (right). These are two *barrier signals* with an element of self-holding and reassurance. They were seen by many children as 'helpful' and 'easy going' respectively, an indication that their significance as signals of uncertainty was not appreciated. Children are not psychic and you should not be too concerned that they are going to pick up your every signal.

Figure 6.14 Normal arms-fold, one of the more assertive barrier signals (right). Self-hold arms-fold, one of a range of comforting self-holding postures (left). Both act as barriers between teacher and class, but the self-hold signals a greater need for reassurance. Both elicited a range of responses from children, but the normal fold tended to be seen more positively (e.g. as 'calm'), while the self-hold fold elicited comments such as 'boring' and 'gets upset'. In this case the element of uncertainty was being picked up.

In assessing the meaning of these signals we have been assuming that they are directed to a large group being taught as a whole. The size of the class will inevitably have some effect on the signals used for gaining attention, both in terms of style and duration. A more intimate group allows a more conversational style. The audience is better able to see subtleties in both gesture and posture and the teacher can try to get responses from 'assembled individuals' rather than a 'group' as such. Feedback is also likely to be more immediate within a smaller group and the teacher will modify her signals, particularly in duration, as she receives responses from her pupils. Even in large groups of polite and enthusiastic adults feedback is very limited, as no individual has responsibility for encouraging the speaker (as would happen in a one-to-one situation), and therefore nobody does it. Pauses in speech, speech volume, facial expressions and gestures are particularly likely to vary with groups of different size.

Figure 6.15 Concentration stares by a group of children. The neutral face and steady stare (left) or neutral mouth and concentration frown, with eyebrows drawn slightly together, are difficult to tell from an expression of anger or irritation, one of the reasons why you may find this illustration disturbing to some extent. In any confrontation the fixed stare is serious, signalling as it does intense disagreement and in some situations an imminent strike! In general conversation, although there will be considerable eye contact, it will include reciprocal and sympathetic gesturing such as nodding, smiling, etc. Where these signals are absent, the intensity suggests suspicion or implied criticism. However, as mentioned above, these feedback signals are normally absent in large groups. This makes the concentration stares of group members seem threatening. You may feel that the boy on the right is more of a risk than the others. His head cant is a signal used from early childhood when questioning another individual. In this case he may be questioning what you are saying because of genuine interest – or, as you may fear, questioning your ability to teach.

The effect that any particular member of the group may be having on you will be due, in part, to your own communication history. Subtleties of head movement, inclination, etc., will be set in the context of the usage that you are familiar with. This is particularly true with regard to different cultures where expression and gesture may have radically different meanings.

Descriptive Exercise – 'An Inspector calls'

Question 1
In any situation, when we are placed under stress most of us will leak the fact, or at least our anxiety, in some way or another. Andy was no exception. His late arrival will have been noticed by the pupils, as will the presence of two relative strangers. This, coupled with his close attention to the file will have indicated that something was not quite normal. The absence of Andy's usual low-level humour was probably noticed as well, and he may have been engaged in some flick checks of his own, this time towards his unwelcome visitors. Glancing at his watch, and paying undue attention to time may have also sent a signal, as would his unusual loudness when calling for the latecomers. The class would have been in no doubt that the circumstances of this lession were unusual, to say the least.

Question 2
The fact that the class eventually responded makes it unlikely that this level of apparent deviancy was the norm. A measure of control was present, but it was not exercised through the usual channels. Shouting, throwing a file to the floor and staring pointedly at the pupils were clear indicators that he had run out of patience. This can be a very quick and effective method of gaining control, but only if it is not the usual one chosen. The class, having been aware that something was amiss, would have had their suspicions confirmed by Andy's reaction, but had this been his normal *modus operandi*, and given that they may have sensed a weakness, they might have run circles round him.

Question 3
Loud noise of any sort, particularly when not expected, will gather the attention of most pupils. Throwing a file to the floor is no exception. Such moves are effective because, unlike language, they have no interpretation in themselves, and in order to make sense of the action more evidence is needed. The pupils will not only be attracted by the dramatic noise but by the intriguing question of what is going to happen next. The facial gestures and postural attitude of the teacher may give some clues, as will the direction and intensity of gaze, but for most pupils actions of this sort are associated with actual or potential loss of temper. Without language to clarify the situation, pupils are unable to judge the risk to their interests. The gamble may just not be worth it!
  It is important to realise, however, that this is merely an attention-getting device; if it is to be effective, it should be reinforced by further action. Andy used several moves to do this. Firstly he pointed to the floor immediately in front of him, gathering the pupils within his space and, therefore, under his authority. Speaking in a quiet and pronounced tone also reinforced his control. Standing, head up and chin out in a particularly dominant way and making eye contact with each pupil in turn, are all likely to add strength to his effort to regain and maintain control.

Question 4
It is always difficult to know how Inspectors think, but this one may well have

considered the first fifteen minutes of Andy's lesson to be, at best, a form of organised chaos. However, the Inspector could not have failed to notice the way in which Andy used his authority to regain control of the lesson, an indication of his awareness and use of status in the establishment and maintenance of classroom control. Andy's recovery was that of a professional who knew his class and his job. A sympathetic Inspector would have understood, and, if he did not approve of the causes of the problem, would have appreciated Andy's response.

Chapter 7

Conveying enthusiasm

Learning is an invisible process which occurs inside children's heads; you can only get access to it indirectly, by asking questions or looking at written work. It is also impossible, with a class of average size, for you to monitor continuously what each child is doing, whether you are trying to teach the whole class or individuals. You cannot force children to learn; you can only persuade them that the work they have to do is a more attractive alternative to the other ways they could spend their time, such as checking their pens or fingernails, discussing last night's video with their friends or seeing how far they can tip their chair without overbalancing. With some classes, some children, or some of the subject-matter you have to teach the best you may be able to do is to make the consequences of these alternatives sufficiently unpleasant that the work is done merely because it is the least of a choice of evils. However, this is at best a wearing strategy, demanding constant vigilance and offering little satisfaction. Arousing the class's interest is far preferable, both practically and intellectually, if it can be achieved.

In order to do this you must do four things. Your manner must convey that the material is interesting and worth making the effort to try to understand; you must relate the material to the children's existing experience so that they can assimilate it to their previous knowledge; and most importantly, you must reward them, rather than criticising them when they try to contribute to the learning process. Finally, you must not disrupt their learning by unnecessarily breaking off teaching and starting disciplinary confrontations when there is no serious threat to the classroom order. While these tasks are common to whole-class work and work with individuals, they are achieved differently in the two situations. We will cover tactics for dealing with individuals in Chapter 9. Determining when a confrontation is not necessary will be dealt with in the next chapter. Much of the art of presenting material interestingly and intelligibly depends on planning decisions made before the start of the lesson, and is outside the area of this book. We raise the matter merely to make the point that only in the most work-oriented classes can you rely on children being prepared to put up with present boredom in the hope of future enlightenment. Generally each step in the subject must be presented so that it interests the children *now*, which depends largely on clear presentation and questioning (Brown and Armstrong 1984, Brown and Edmondson 1984). Clear planning and ordering of topics can assist this, but much depends on presentation.

WHAT THE EFFECTIVE TEACHERS DID

We will look first at how the effective teachers in our video study (Neill 1991a) differed from their less effective peers, both across the lessons overall and during their talk about the subject, and then consider some of these aspects in more detail. We used a very strict definition, only counting times when the teachers were actually talking about the subject, and excluding questions to the class, the class's replies, talk about lesson administration, and so on. Only 16 per cent of the lessons was included on this strict criterion, but teachers' behaviour during this talk was very much like their talk over the lesson as a whole – not surprisingly, considering the firm subject-orientation of the lessons.

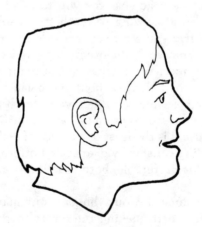

Figure 7.1 Head forward and smile, a relatively mild expression of interest in what the child has to say. Most children saw this teacher as 'friendly', or gave a mixture of other positive comments

The most striking feature of the effective teachers was their enthusiasm and decisiveness. We shall quote some sections of Mr Weathering's lesson below. He was a senior teacher, and had probably taught classes about weathering fifty or a hundred times before, and had known the elementary concepts of weathering he was discussing for maybe thirty years. However, his reception of the boys' initial answers as they groped towards the concepts suggested that he was receiving the most exciting revelations since Noah first thought of the Ark (Figures 7.1, 7.2 and 7.5). He literally seemed to be hanging on their every word; this was characteristic of popular and effective teachers. Mr Integral, another of this group, greeted his slow-learners' steps towards the mathematical conception of speed with a reverential 'Magic!' The enthusiasm might seem overdone, but thirteen-year-olds do live in a more vivid world than adults, and what might seem restrained to an adult audience seems downright boring to them. A less exaggerated response would be appropriate with older classes.

Figure 7.2 The forward lean, smile, and slight head cant (i.e. head at an angle), indicate attention to and positive feelings about the child. The teacher is also nominating the child to speak, in this case by pointing. Most children saw this teacher as 'helpful' or 'friendly'

How did the effective teachers actually convey their enthusiasm? We found that over the lessons as a whole, effective teachers used a wider variety of facial expressions, gestures and tones of voice. The difference was particularly marked for illustrative gestures and animated and imitative intonation which made the lesson material more interesting and vivid for the class. We also found the effective teachers looked intently at the class more often than the others, and used head movements (head forward, Figure 7.1; head cant, Figure 7.2; and head dip) which are signals of involvement with a speaker: they thus showed their keen interest in what the children had to say when they contributed to the lesson. Effective teachers smiled more, and used more joking intonation; their lessons were more fun to be in. Very much the same picture occurred during the actual educational talk (though not the joking), but effective teachers spent more time discussing hypotheses than the ineffective ones – in other words, their lessons were more intellectually stimulating. The ineffective teachers may have been unable to spend time in this way because they could not command the attention of the class for a long continuous period; they were also spending more time dealing with materials and in unclassified talk. (Rapid and efficient organisation of the class was recognised by Kounin (1970) as a mark of the effective teacher.) This was indicated by the effective teachers' greater use of controlling signals, such as the batons (Figure 6.11) and fend (Figure 7.3), which showed their decisive approach. Teachers must be in control of their classes as well as interesting them, and these behaviours are the way in which the effective teachers convey this.

Figure 7.3 Palm forward (left) and palm down (right) two controlling gestures. They indicate, respectively, that the class should stop or calm down. Most children gave negative responses, especially 'strict'

Ineffective teachers' behaviour was notable for uncertainty. They showed this by using more barrier signals (Figure 6.5) over the lessons as a whole, and fumbling with their clothes more (Figures 6.6, 6.7) when they were actually talking about the subject. They spent less time with their hands in their pockets, a signal of relaxation, and when they were talking they stood still less. As we mentioned in the last chapter, uncertain people show a variety of stereotyped swaying, rocking or pacing movements, which are intention movements of escape, and lead to their being seen as ineffectual. Both over the lessons as a whole and during educational talk, the ineffective teachers spent more time with a neutral facial expression than the effective ones, and during educational talk they used neutral intonation much more: their performance came across as flat. No wonder they occasionally looked sad when talking! Whereas effective teachers spent a majority of their educational talk time with individual children, ineffective teachers spent much less time in this way, losing an opportunity to build up a rapport with the class by relating to them individually.

Overall, the ineffective teachers' problem in dealing with their classes seems to have been their lack of confidence, which prevented them from achieving the warm but dominant role which seems necessary for the lower secondary age-groups. This does not mean that they were not pleasant and caring people – in fact the problem often seemed to be that they were too involved with and attached to their children and their subject, so much so that they found inattention and disinterest threatening and depressing. They lacked that degree of detachment which would have allowed them to give a good performance, even to an initially sceptical audience.

THE CLASS AND THEIR ATTITUDE TO THE SUBJECT

Most classes will enter the classroom for the first time neither knowing what they have to learn, nor interested in it. You, however, have spent some years studying your subject for its own sake, and chose it because you were interested in it yourself. You know how the material you are teaching today fits into the overall structure of the subject. Your pupils are being taken for a compulsory route-march into the unknown, at an age when they do not have a clear enough appreciation of the future to really appreciate any assurance you give them of the future usefulness of what they are doing. It is an exaggeration to say that most children never develop an interest in subjects for their own sake, but it is a useful exaggeration. Even the most academic children place a heavy emphasis on the opinions of their peers when interviewed, followed by their relationship with the teacher (Turner 1983). You must therefore arrange things so that every step is rewarding *at the time it is taken*, without relying on the children's willingness to accept present penance in the hope of future salvation. Some of them may be willing to do so; but they are not the ones who are going to make your life difficult.

We have already discussed the kinds of signals which children use to gain each others' attention and support; we have suggested that children act in these ways to build up and maintain their self-esteem. If the more assertive members of your class want to get the attention of others, they can do it by disrupting the class, enraging the teacher, and getting a reputation for daring (Beynon 1985). More positively, they can also do it by contributing disproportionately to the classroom discussion. For example, during the first week of the video study, Kevin was a conspicuous member of his new second-year class; he was one of the first to volunteer to answer questions in virtually every subject. The most striking example was in Home Economics, where he displayed a complete knowledge of every type of cooking utensil and technique; if any of the girls had ever been in a kitchen, she got little opportunity to expand on it. Kevin was big and mature for his age; why did he try to identify himself so conspicuously with what might have been thought an 'unsuitable' subject for a growing boy? We can only conclude that the end justified the means; provided he could contribute effectively to the class he was willing to take the risk of ridicule. In other classes where either he was denied the same chance of self-expression, or the subject matter was too difficult for him to be able to succeed immediately, he started to behave more disruptively.

Should children be allowed to behave in this way? Why should Kevin ramble on about pots and pans, to the exclusion of other class members? Shouldn't every member of the class be given equal attention? We don't have any hard information on how this domination of the class by one or two individuals develops, but the clear impression from our limited sample is that where the teacher allows a dominant child to make his mark in a productive way in early sessions, his influence, though still strong, becomes less conspicuous in later sessions. Once he has decided that disruption is the most desirable way for him to express his influence, however, his influence is likely to continue at a high level – if only because the teacher is constantly forced to do something about him if she wants to get anything taught. Better to allow him to influence the class in a more positive way. Ideally, to be sure, you would like him to contribute from pure love of the subject, but if he contributes from love of the sound of his own voice, this is probably better than the alternatives.

In the hands of many experienced teachers, the first lesson takes a rather special form. Moskowitz and Hayman (1974, 1976) found that 'best' teachers used it mainly to get the relationship between class and teacher going, rather than to get moving on the subject. New teachers, however, plunged straight into the subject; after the honeymoon period they found their relationships with the class and the amount of work they could get done pursuing a steady downward course. We will come back to how you can use non-verbal and verbal behaviour to express interest in all your children as persons and in their contributions after first considering the rather special tactics of the first lesson.

THE FIRST LESSON – MAKING CONTACT WITH THE SUBJECT

In many cases, the teachers who went on to form effective relationships with their classes started the first lesson, after a brief introduction to the term's work, by asking what the children already knew of the area, first in general, and then specifically in relation to the topic of the first lesson. What did they know about the First World War? How did it start? What is physical geography? How can the earth's crust change? What are the types of weathering? Who saw the athletics last night? How far did they run? How long did they take? How could we tell how fast they were running?

While this approach tells the teacher what the class already know, it is probably more important in suggesting to the children that you are interested in them and their knowledge, and in giving the more assertive members of the class a chance to be involved, as we have already mentioned. If you are alert, you may be able to deduce a considerable amount about the social structure of the class during the process. In some cases, the teacher had a stand-alone lesson which did not even start the main course which was going to be developed through the term. One 'best' teacher of English, for example, got his class to discuss and write about 'memorable teachers'. This was related to the book they were going to read, but its main function was to get across that he was aware of the way they saw teachers, that he was 'one of the boys' (it was a single-sex school) and to give him a chance to go round the class to get to know them.

The less successful teachers either did not take this approach, or if they did, failed to build up their relationship with the class. For example, one Geography teacher, who was going to go on to land-use maps, started by taking the class round the school to map what happened in each part of the building. Potentially this was a splendid idea;

the class were new to the school, and they could quickly learn information which they might otherwise have taken a long time to pick up, suffering the embarrassment of displaying their ignorance on the way. They could get practical experience of the concepts of usage mapping in a way which they were likely to remember. However, the exercise turned into a game of hide-and-seek around the building, because he could not exert adequate dominance, and it is doubtful whether the children gained much related to the subject. It is not enough to be well-meaningly nice; it is also necessary to control the interaction so that children get the encouragement they need to participate and the discouragement they need to avoid being disruptive. Here we will look only at the encouraging side; discouraging tactics come in Chapter 8.

EXPRESSING INTEREST IN CHILDREN

Inevitably, in asking questions, you will receive relevant answers and complete red herrings, as well as answers which take you further in the direction you plan to go. You will also receive answers which are so complete that if you accept them and go on from them, many of the class will be left behind, so you must partially backtrack until you are sure most have grasped the point. As we have said, from your viewpoint, questions may be related primarily to building up the academic structure, or the ethos, of the subject, while the children are partly or wholly unaware of this structure or ethos, and of the long term; from their point of view, immediate outcomes are what counts. Every time a child volunteers an answer he risks making a fool of himself in front of his peers: if his incomplete or over-complete answer is rejected, especially during initial contact with a teacher, he is unlikely to be so keen to risk his self-esteem again. (Once the relationship is established, you can afford to be somewhat more rejecting, providing you are not too unpleasant about it.) The effective teachers were very skilled at ensuring that children were rescued from potential embarrassment. To do this you need to allow the child time to collect his thoughts, to provide cues or repeat the question, to show interest with your non-verbal behaviour and to praise rather than criticise. Here is an example from the first lesson in Geography described above. Mr Weathering is asking the boys what they understand by 'physical geography' and has elicited a string of examples: 'hills', 'rivers', 'the shape of the earth'; finally he gets:

> *Boy:*   The crust.
> *Mr Weathering:*   What do you mean by the crust?
> *Boy:*   The inside. [*Giggle from the rest of the class.*]
> *Mr Weathering* [*moving towards him, with a surprised smile*]: Now, where is the crust on a loaf of bread?
> *Boy:*   Er – on the outside.
> *Mr Weathering:*   Right. Now the crust – and that's a good word, that's the [*emphasising it by tone of voice*] **technical** term we use – is changing all the time. Can anybody tell me a time when it will change very rapidly?

Not only is the boy not criticised for his *faux pas*, but he is rescued from the ridicule of the rest of the class by praise for having produced the correct technical term. Mr Weathering is getting across that he will make sure that any attempt to genuinely contribute to the progress of the lesson will earn its contributor credit. Later in the school year, when the relationship had stabilised, he could express this verbally; when a boy failed to make a fairly simple calculation about population growth:

Figure 7.4 'Devilish' face, indicating pleasure in inflicting pain. Children saw this face as 'friendly' or 'fun', not noticing the expression in the eyebrows

> *Mr Weathering* [*with a 'devilish smile' (Figure 7.4), pointing finger and humorously emphatic intonation*]: You've fallen **right in the trap**! [*Quickly, moving towards boy*]: Go on, save yourself!

The opposite problem occurs when one child has jumped ahead of the rest of the class in his understanding. How are you to get the rest of the class to the same point without contrasting their lack of understanding unfavourably with the full answer you have just received, or seeming to discard the effort of the child who has tried to respond? In his first lesson, shortly after the incident described above, Mr Weathering moved on from the definition of 'physical geography' to a first discussion of some of its content. Earthquakes are rapidly mentioned, but when Mr Weathering asks how they are caused, he gets too complete an answer:

> *Mr Weathering*:   What is actually **happening** when you have an earthquake?
> *Boy*:   Sir?
> [*Mr Weathering turns and orients, looking intently towards him*].
> *Boy*:   Sir, there's a fault under the ground.
> *Mr Weathering*:   Yeah, I'm **ignorant** [*turning both hands to point to his chest and with a puzzled frown*] I'm only a geographer and not a geologist, so I don't understand that, right?

[Looking intently at the boy with a puzzled frown]: Now what do you mean when you say that there's a fault underneath the ground? *[Looking round the class and making juggling movements with his cupped hands]*: You're all talking in *technical* terms and I don't understand the technical terms. What's a **fault**?

Boy: *[slightly hesitantly; Mr Weathering resumes his concentrated attention to him]*: Something that happens under the ground, right . . . it goes kind of sideways . . . and breaks the earth up.

Mr Weathering [rocking his head from side to side and looking upwards]. **Good**. Right, so you're putting a lot of ideas together there. *[Reorienting towards boy]* So we're talking about a crack in the ground, are we? *[Gazing intently towards boy.]*

Boy: Yes sir.

Mr Weathering: A big 'un or a little 'un?

Boy: A big 'un.

Mr Weathering: How big?

Boy: Um . . .

Mr Weathering   [Looking round, beginning to turn to rest of class and gesture]: Right, he says there's a crack in the ground. *[Rapidly]* It might be a sort of crack in the concrete like the one outside my back door or what they did at Cresswell [House] last week when they drove that bulldozer down the pavement. Does he **mean** that sort of crack?

Various members of the class: No . . . Sir! Sir!

Again Mr Weathering is supportive, through his sustained and intense attention and emphasis on the technical correctness of the answers, and this compensates for the fact that he first requires the boy to extend and explain his original contribution, and then redirects the question to other members of the class. He thus manages to extend the discussion of the point until he is sure that all members of the class have understood what he is talking about, without causing offence to the boy who answers first.

Intonation and silence

In looking at the non-verbal indications of enthusiasm, we cannot omit the non-verbal components of speech. You emphasise your interest *paralinguistically* by a wide range in the tempo, pitch and loudness of your speech, drawing attention to the features of the children's contributions which you think are especially important, as we have hinted in the examples from Mr Weathering's lesson above. The importance of intonation in classroom talk has been well covered by Sinclair and Brazil (1982) and Brazil *et al.* (1980), and its subtleties cannot be adequately covered in a small space. A brief quote however, will indicate what it can convey. Ms Hola's class are writing out the present tense of the Spanish verb *tener*, which is used in various idioms which are new to them; but they have known the verb for some time.

Ms Hola: What letter does *tenie* end with?

Class: With an i.

Ms Hola: With an **i**?

Class: With an e.
Ms Hola: With an **e**.

The plain print gives no hint of the quality of this exchange. Ms Hola stresses the 'i' heavily, and her rising pitch conveys an almost scornful incredulity at the class's ignorance; when they supply the right answer, the stress and slurred falling pitch on the 'e' reinforce the reminder that they should have known this all along. Overall, her tone is low-pitched, rather than the higher pitch which would indicate annoyance; within six words and as many seconds she has demonstrated a firm but humorous control over her class.

However, it is not only talk which is important; you must also know when to keep silent. When you ask a question, you must allow an adequate *wait time* for the child to answer. In normal conversation speakers pause as they speak, to collect their thoughts about what they are going to say next, and this is accentuated when children speak in the classroom because they often find the answers difficult, and because of their subordinate position relative to the teacher, and the fact that they are being put on the spot publicly. Adults in normal conversational situations have a range of tactics for 'holding the floor' during their pauses for thought (Beattie 1983), but children in classroom situations do not seem very effective at this, either because their conversational skills are not yet fully developed, or, more probably, because the social setting, responding to a dominant questioner with other members of the class trying to butt in, is too inhibiting. Considerable skill is needed to give one child a fair chance without frustrating others. Rowe (1974) showed that children produce answers with substantial silences (often of over three seconds) embedded in them. Children seemed to collect their thoughts in silence for the first section of their answers; after producing this, they then needed another silence to collect the next section, continuing the pattern of silent thought and bursts of speech until their contribution was complete. Teachers tended to jump in during the silences (on average they waited only 0.9 seconds), either trying to hurry the child up or diverting the question to another child, so that the first child was allowed no answer, or only part of the answer that he could have worked through, given the chance. Not surprisingly, children found this frustrating and felt they were valued far more by teachers who had longer wait times and allowed them to give the answers of which they were capable.

You can encourage the child to hold the floor by giving him your undivided attention. First, you can keep your gaze on him, rather than scanning around for someone else who might have a better answer. Second, you can signal by leaning towards him, nodding or smiling. If you are genuinely interested you will do this spontaneously. The lean can take a mild form, with just the head forward (Figures 7.1, 7.3), or go to the extreme of 'catching' the child's idea, like a wicket-keeper (Figure 7.5). This may seem rather theatrical, but bolder movements are appropriate with a large audience – the hand gestures described below, for example, are frequently used by forceful lecturers to adult audiences. The extra assertiveness makes up for the less immediate contact each member of a large audience has with the speaker, in comparison to participants in a one-to-one conversation. In addition, children's conversations are often much more animated than those of adults – a comparison of the break-time conversations in the corridor or playground with those in the staffroom will make the point.

Figure 7.5 Here the teacher is effectively miming 'catching' the idea which the child is producing in her answer, with a more extreme forward lean. Most children saw this teacher positively, e.g as 'helpful', but some children may find this type of approach overpowering

CONTROLLING A DISCUSSION

In order to allow one child to make his contribution, you will have to stop others interrupting, and nominate those whose turn it is to speak. Just as childrens' conversations are more animated than those of adults, so are the rivalries between their cliques; this poses problems, especially if you are trying to organise discussions among groups of younger adolescents. Discussions, as you may have experienced them on your own training course, depend critically on all concerned accepting the value of ideas contributed, regardless of who contributes them. Children tend to assess the value of an idea in terms of the person who contributed it; they may reject ideas from children of whom they have a low opinion, or interrupt them while they are speaking. Alternatively they may simply lose interest in the discussion while other children are speaking, and find some alternative pursuit. Many children do not regard discussions as 'real' work (e.g. Furlong 1976), so they may give them a low level of attention to start with. All this means that you will not only need to act as chairman in any discussion lesson, but you will usually need to do so in a fairly formal way. If the class is cooperative, or you have built up a good relationship with them, more spontaneous discussion is possible. It is likely that spontaneous discussions will be dominated by a small proportion of the class, like Kevin, mentioned earlier, who are dominant in the peer group (Macpherson 1983). This tendency is apparent in any spontaneous discussion group (for instance a seminar group of adults, but much less obviously, because adults are more polite). You will probably have difficulty in preventing it if the discussion is to remain spontaneous. You may not even be aware of it, because of the pace at which events proceed; and, as we have suggested, it may not be desirable to try to work against the social pressures of the class. This has to be a question of judgement; at least in low-achieving classes, it is likely that those who are most willing to contribute will not be those best-qualified academically to do so. Even so, the class as a whole may learn more if they contribute than if you are constantly having to fend them off from disrupting a discussion led by the more academic.

If you choose a more teacher-structured discussion, you will need to nominate participants by name, or by pointing to them (Figure 7.2). You can also use a range of more subtle signals, such as an eyebrow flash, an upward flick or forward thrust of the head, or a head cant (Figure 7.6). You will also need to enforce silence by a palm-forward or palm-down gesture, while nominating the child you want to speak (Figure 7.3).

Figure 7.6 Head cant, an expression of close attention which first appears in pre-school children. The position may be held, while the teacher gazes steadily at the child, or the teacher may use it as a brief head-flick, to nominate a child to speak

Gestures; or do you see what I mean?

It may seem paradoxical to consider ways of asking children questions before looking at the ways of telling them about the subject, but we have done this for three reasons. First, as an antidote to the tendency of inexperienced teachers to talk on when they should be involving the class more. Second, because especially in initial lessons, questioning allows you to discover the initial conceptual framework which the children possess and allows the children to realise that their new knowledge can be connected to their existing knowledge. Third, because questioning can demonstrate your interest in and involvement with individuals more easily than even interesting and humorous talk to the class. Talking to individual children is a good way of showing your interest in them, but you can only spend time on individual talk when the class have been settled down. Individual talk is a subject for the next chapter; we now turn to the ways you can show enthusiasm when talking to the whole class.

Experienced teachers use a great variety of gestures when talking to classes (and are often appalled to see themselves on video). All these gestures appear in normal conversation, especially when one speaker is putting forward a difficult or forceful argument. It is also possible to see children start to use them as soon as they find themselves putting a public case to the class as a whole (provided they are not inhibited by the novelty of the situation), or when discussing something avidly with their friends.

There are several types of gesture (McNeill 1985) . The first type, generally called 'emblems', such as the V-sign, have a generally known equivalent verbal meeting; being mostly insult signs, they should have little currency in orderly classrooms. More important in classrooms are gestures which serve to illustrate, amplify and punctuate speech. These gestures confirm what you are saying, firstly by showing the shapes or movements of objects (*iconix*), secondly by miming the concept you are talking about, or your educational intention (*metaphorix*) and thirdly by directing the children's attention to salient parts of the message (*beats*). In McNeill's view, all three types of gesture originate from the same thought processes as speech; the message is then processed through verbal and non-verbal channels, which may confirm and duplicate each other, or provide complementary information. In other words, your gestures give your class a second chance to receive your message. As we shall see, if you are uncertain, your gestures can cut you off from your audience; and if their cultural background is very different to your own, they may have problems with your gestural language as well as your verbal language.

Children's gestures do not reach the fully adult form until after twelve, though most of the adult features are present by nine or ten. Children of this age are likely to be more influenced by gestures than younger ones, who respond more to the words. A five-year-old's gestures indicate the child's high level of involvement in what he is talking about, reflecting the egocentric state of his thought processes; older children and adults use more abstract gestures, indicating detachment from the topic of discussion (McNeill 1986). Younger children act out their topic; older children and adults observe it.

Iconix merge into pointing (Figure 7.7) and miming in younger children. They

Figure 7.7 Finger point (left) is more precise than the palm point (right); it is also used (rather more frequently than the palm point) when precise items, rather than general aspects are being pointed out on the board

demonstrate where something is, or show the shape of something, either concrete, like the First World War trenches, or more abstract, like the 'shape' of an equation (Figure 7.8). In some cases, such as the trenches just mentioned, much of the meaning may be transmitted through the gesture. Metaphorix signify abstract ideas, such as mathematical concepts, which cannot be directly represented as physical forms, but are nevertheless illustrated by spatial analogies. Most importantly in the teaching situation, these gestures point out to the class how they should react to what you are saying, by showing them the kind of information you are trying to communicate to them. You offer ideas to the class or reach out to them (Figure 7.9), hold ideas up for the class to see (Figure 7.10), open the door to a new idea (Figure 7.10), break through a barrier of possible confusion (Figure 7.11) or emphasise the precision with which an idea must be grasped (Figure 7.12).

In the same way, effective teachers use facial expressions to signal to the class how they should react to the material the teacher is discussing; when it is interesting they raise their brows (Figure 7.13), when it is difficult they concentrate (Figure 7.14), and at exceptionally difficult points they look puzzled (Figure 7.15). Again there is evidence that expressions are used in the same way outside the teaching situation. A puzzled expression (Figure 7.15) is used in conversations to convey that the speaker still wishes to hold the floor, and is silent because she cannot think of the right word, not because

Figure 7.8 An effective teacher miming the course of the First World War trenches down between Belgium and Switzerland

her contribution to the conversation has ended. The puzzled expression serves to show the listener that a contribution to the speaker's chain of meaning may be acceptable, but a deviation to the listener's interest will not be. In the less equal social situation of the classroom, these expressions serve to alert the class to attend to your definition of the situation.

Gestures are also used to punctuate and shape conversation; McNeill calls these gestures *beats*. Beats are jerky movements which are made at the ends of phrases – corresponding to the punctuation marks in writing, and serving the same purpose. In conversations between adults, gesture can be used to regulate the attention of the listener to the speaker. By gesturing, the speaker ensures that the listener's attention is on her before she delivers her verbal message, avoiding the risk that it will be missed or that it will have to be repeated. This function can also be served by verbal markers; in the classroom these, together with other conspicuous means of getting attention, are

Figure 7.9 The palm up, which offers an idea to the class. Children saw this teacher positively, e.g as 'interesting' or 'helpful'

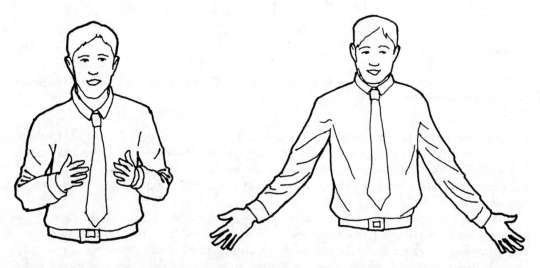

Figure 7.10 Air hold (left) and open sesame (right) batons. The air hold presents an idea to the class; the teacher is effectively holding it up for their inspection. The open sesame often occurs in a less extreme form than shown here; the arms sweep to the open position, usually from an air hold. It is used at the end of an explanation; the teacher signals to the class that the ideas he has been presenting should now be clearly accessible to them

Figure 7.11 Air punch (left), a forceful gesture used to make a point strongly, either while explaining to children or when disciplining them. Air chop (right), cutting through a difficult problem to a solution

more commonly used than in ordinary speech, because of the difficulty of organising the joint attention of a whole class (Chapter 6).

However, in informal conversations, self-directed gestures can serve to break off interaction, especially when the hand grooms or covers the face (Figure 6.8) – grooming other parts of the body does not seem to have this effect. (This is a less extreme version of the *cut-off*, used, as its name implies, when one wants to avoid a situation completely – a familiar example being when people hide their faces from something horrifying on television.) Such signals, which we found were more frequently shown by ineffective teachers, were literally acting as barriers between them and their classes. However, self-directed gestures can have a positive function, too. Teachers not infrequently use these gestures when questioning children, and they may serve to clarify that responsibility for continuing the classroom dialogue is being passed over from the usually dominant teacher to the child. By cutting off your own signal, you can give your pupils a space to make their contributions.

As mentioned above, children's gestures develop in phase with their speech, and young children do not understand the more abstract adult gestures. Their understanding of gestures develops in parallel with their production. Perhaps fortunately for teachers, children's potential to be influenced by gestures because they understand them develops in parallel with the teacher's need to overcome their resistance to learn! As an inexperienced teacher, you need not therefore worry about your ability to

Figure 7.12 Counting off points as they are made verbally; teachers also sometimes use an erratic sideways sweep of both hands miming the form of a sentence, when the sense requires that the class follows through the implications of a particular point

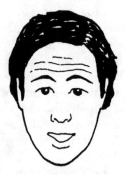

Figure 7.13 Brow raise, an expression of interest, which also occurs as a brief 'eyebrow flash'. It is used extensively by many teachers to signal that they are talking about something which should interest the class. Like the following two expressions, this is used by teachers to involve the class socially, by indicating what is an acceptable reaction from the children

Figure 7.14 Concentration frown; this expression is ambiguous and could be mild anger; but the context of the teacher's speech will make clear that he is discussing material which should be seen as difficult

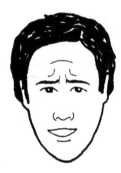

Figure 7.15 Puzzle frown; like the concentration frown, it is used as a signal when the teacher has just asked a difficult question which the children need think about; the teacher, of course, usually already knows the answer

produce these gestures and expressions; you will already have a complete repertoire from your existing conversational experience. Further, the signals happen so rapidly that they are not normally under conscious control, unlike the longer-lasting dominant postures described in the previous chapters. Their satisfactory appearance depends on your being at ease both with your subject-matter and your class, so that you start to gesture spontaneously to fit your expansive mood. Lack of gestures indicates lack of involvement with and mastery of the ideas being communicated and thus gives a clear signal to the class that you are not on top of your subject. If you are uncertain you will tend to show the barrier or displacement signals described in the previous chapter, closing in on yourself, when you should be opening out with gestures.

Avoiding hesitancy

If you are uncertain and showing a closed posture, accompanying this will probably be a flat or querulous tone of voice, conveying a lack of confidence and interest in the subject; and you will probably need to hesitate frequently to collect your thoughts. We have mentioned this pattern of halts earlier, together with repetitions and looking away from the person spoken to, when we discussed Rowe's work on children's answers. In a public speaking context, hesitations indicate uncertainty and reduce credibility.

Hesitation results from your need to process each section of speech before you produce it. You can reduce this need in two ways. First, you must ensure thorough familiarity with your subject matter, so you have less processing to do at the time you are teaching. If you have freedom to choose your own lesson content, you should, until you have settled into a relationship with the class, pick topics which you know extremely well and find fascinating, so that your grasp of your subject and your enthusiasm for it can be transmitted to the class. Except in subjects like Mathematics, where particular topics may have to be taught at the start of the year because they are prerequisites for the understanding of other material, it may be better to avoid introductory or foundation topics which, while technically important, make boring lessons – for the short time until you have established rapport with the class. Where you have to teach to a fixed curriculum, you will have the advantage that colleagues have already covered the topics at the same point in previous years, and will be able to advise you on the best approach. There may well be texts or hand-outs, and the class may itself know what it is due to be taught. Your position will also be strengthened because you are integrated into the school's overall plan of work.

Second, where possible you must break down the material into small chunks, rather than giving one long lecture. Here questions show their value again. By working through an idea in a series of questions to the class, you throw much of the information-processing burden on to the children – but make sure to support them in the ways we have mentioned. You now have to handle only the formulation of the questions, and expansion and clarification of the children's answers. The material is also covered at a slower pace, which makes it easier for the children to grasp. In these ways you should avoid appearing hesitant and confused, and you should be able to convey enthusiasm for both your subject and your class. You can then reasonably demand that the children show equal enthusiasm.

SUMMARY

Enthusiastic teachers use a wide range of facial expressions, intonation and gestures to convey the interest and excitement of the subject matter. This is necessary, especially in the first lesson, because many pupils will not be inherently interested in the subject. For such pupils, the teacher's personal interest in them and their contribution will be their main motivation. You can express interest by signals such as attentive orientation and gaze, sufficient wait time to allow the pupil to organise his answer without interruption, and supportive responses to errors, at least in initial encounters.

Enthusiastic speakers use gestures (iconix and metaphorix) as a supportive channel to speech, primarily to indicate how the audience should interpret the ideas being presented verbally. Gestures can also carry part of the substantive meaning, and the audience can be compelled to pay closer attention by switching content from speech to gesture. Facial expression can also serve this function. On the other hand, hesitancy diminishes the audience's confidence in the speaker; to avoid it you need to know your material thoroughly and to structure it well.

The training materials look at signs of enthusiasm – or lack of it – displayed by speaker and audience, to stimulate discussion on how teachers can involve their classes. They also consider the type of lesson which an experienced teacher may give which would fail to enthuse her class.

TRAINING MATERIALS

If you heard an effective and popular teacher leave the staffroom with the comment, 'I'm just off to conduct another lesson', you would probably be safe in taking her words literally. Enthusiasm is conveyed with the whole body, using facial expression, gesture and movement to create, develop and punctuate the lesson in a way that involves the audience, willing or conscripted.

Most adults have a well-defined range of such gestures and movements, but within a potentially difficult environment, like a classroom, it may be more a question of knowing when and which ones to use. There is no better way for seeing how enthusiasm is conveyed than to watch an enthusiast in action. Look around the staffroom at colleagues who are describing holidays, their hobby, or the absence of a notorious pupil from their lesson, and you will see the visual language of enthusiasm in action.

Pictorial Exercise – 'Encore!'

Conveying enthusiasm through posture, gesture and expression is a more or less continuous process, yet somewhat difficult to illustrate from a snapshot in time.

There are, however, certain clearly defined signals which, although they are often quickly developed and embroidered by classroom interaction, serve to gather and maintain the audience's attention.

Question 1   The images portrayed in Figures 7.16–7.19 could be seen at the beginning of almost any lesson. Assume for the moment that you are the one on the receiving end. Would you feel inclined to take note of any of these people, and if so, why? How are they displaying their enthusiasm?

Question 2   Reverse the position. You are presenting a lesson and find yourself greeted by the expressions shown in Figures 7.20–7.23. What is your immediate assessment of their meaning? What techniques are available to you to involve these listeners further?

Figure 7.16

Figure 7.17

Figure 7.18

Figure 7.19

Figure 7.20

Figure 7.21

Figure 7.22

Figure 7.23

Descriptive exercise – 'All or nothing'

The school in which Mrs Adamant teaches has developed a new policy to ensure that all pupils in the school receive pastoral support and a personal and social education programme. This is to be taught during a specified period of the day. All the teachers in the school are to teach it, irrespective of their specialities and preferred subject areas. During the early INSET for the programme several teachers had expressed their concern that they felt that they did not possess the necessary knowledge or skills to put across the programme that had been designed for them.

Mrs Adamant was particularly concerned as, although an experienced teacher, she rarely had lessons with a discussion content in her subject area. She normally ensured that pupils did a substantial amount of technical and written work. During the first lesson Mrs Adamant was told to cover the topic of 'friendship'. She had prepared the teaching materials, which included some reading material, in advance. Mrs Adamant introduced the lesson, telling the class that this was a lesson that they had to do because the school had decided that it was good for them. She handed out the materials and, reading from her copy, which was placed directly on the table in front of her, she read through the instructions, never once lifting her eyes from the sheet. The majority of the class followed with her, and paid reasonable attention to her instructions as to how they should head the paper and rule the margins.

Mrs Adamant looked at her watch and noted that the class had some twenty-five minutes in which to complete the work. She informed them of this and then told them to begin, and that they could discuss the issues in pairs, if they wished to, but to keep the noise level to a minimum.

The class worked relatively quietly, in some cases copying charts and filling them in with their own answers. During this period Mrs Adamant walked around the class looking at the work that the students were producing, but only by looking over their shoulders and always at a distance.

By the second lesson on 'friendship', the class were getting restless. Again, most were working quietly, but others had begun talking, and not always about the work in question. Mrs Adamant remained seated at her desk for most of this lesson, until asked a question by one pupil, the question being, 'Miss, do teachers have friends in the staffroom like we have friends in the playground, or do you only work with each other?' Mrs Adamant's response was an honest one and she talked for a short while about the nature of relationships in a staffroom. She noticed as she did so that the class became very interested in what she was saying; soon they were all listening and were beginning to ask supplementary questions. Mrs Adamant moved around and leant against the front of the desk. As she discussed the topic with the pupils she directed her conversation far more to them as individuals. She began to use gesture and expression more and noticed, as if by accident, that humour began to creep in to some of her replies. The pupils joined in in a very controlled and light-hearted way, and soon, more quickly than she had planned, the lesson came to an end.

Mrs Adamant returned to the staffroom and immediately announced that the lesson had been the best that she had taught in the new pastoral programme.

Question 1   By Mrs Adamant's own definition had she, in fact, 'taught' the second lesson in the accepted sense of the word?

Question 2   Why do you think that the pupils had so readily responded to Mrs Adamant's replies about the staffroom?

Question 3   Clearly, Mrs Adamant became more relaxed when talking confidently about the topic. What non-verbal signals would you have expected Mrs Adamant to have used during that series of enthusiastic replies?

Question 4   Why did Mrs Adamant's relaxed stance have such an impact on the class, and how could she capitalize on this in future lessons?

TRAINING MATERIALS – ANSWERS TO EXERCISES

Figure 7.16 A leaning-back posture and sad expression indicate mild depression or fear. This is drawn from a video of an unsuccessful lesson; the teacher is watching the class irreverently file out. Her disappointment and her knowledge that her chances of improving the outcome are limited are apparent. Children were undecided about this teacher; she was most often described as 'boring'. Since 'boring' teachers are seen as fair game, her premonition of future trouble would be justified. Similar reactions were given to other behaviour patterns indicating uncertainty.

Figure 7.17 Air purse, expressing the precision of an idea; used when it is important that the class concentrate to take in an important point. This is a 'vacuum' version of the precision grip used metaphorically to grasp small objects. This gesture seems especially characteristic of Mathematics teachers, relating to the nature of the subject. Cultures vary in their use of gestures of the types shown in this and the next two figures, and pupils from some language backgrounds may not be helped in their understanding by such gestures. There is little you can do about this, except to take other steps to ensure they do understand.

Figure 7.18 The palm side indicates a desire to reach out to the class and get them to go along with the teacher's view. Again, this is a metaphorical use of an originally functional movement.

Figure 7.19 The palm back gesture, usually used when the teacher is trying to get the class to embrace an idea. It may also be miming drawing the pupils closer to the teacher. Most children saw this teacher positively, especially as 'friendly'.

Figure 7.20 Gazing out of the window or into space represents a closed challenge. He may actually be thinking how he should tackle the next section of the task, or be distracted by a passing incident outside. In either case he will revert to his work without prompting, and the teacher should not intervene. However, if the teacher notices he continually does this, it constitutes a closed challenge, and the teacher needs to intervene in a non-threatening way, perhaps by approaching him to talk about the work and offer help.

Figure 7.21 You may assume that the relaxed backward lean and head-prop, with a fixed gaze either at the teacher or into space, represents boredom. It would do so in a one-to-one conversation, where the listener continually encourages and reinforces the speaker. As a member of a large group, the pupil does not have this responsibility. If his gaze is on the teacher, his relaxation is only to be expected in the course of a long lesson. However, the posture may develop into a closed challenge if his attention wanders, and even into an open challenge if he tips his chair back, grins to his friends and starts making control checks.

Figure 7.22 This posture is more assertive than Figure 7.21; the forward lean implies a willingness to get involved, and the overt head-prop indicates boredom. However, at this stage the threat to liven things up is only a mild one and may never come near to being converted into action. Provided her gaze is steady, and she reacts appropriately when the teacher makes a joke or a point which needs to be written down, her level of attention is satisfactory. If she is not responding, action will be needed to draw her back into the lesson.

Figure 7.23   Slight differences in posture make this a more direct challenge. The elbow on the back of the chair and the forceful lean on the other hand (note the pressure line on his cheek) suggest a more 'posed' posture. He is also closer to the teacher than the girl in the previous picture (note the perspective of the desk), and at this distance the direct gaze is more challenging. If this was a closed challenge we would expect him to break gaze as the teacher came close, rather than continuing to glare up under his brows.

Descriptive Exercise – 'All or nothing'

Question 1
Mrs Adamant may have felt a fraud to some extent, owing to the fact that by her definition a lesson is only a lesson if the children are writing down facts and remembering them. Here, however, she was introduced to a new dimension. Teaching a successful lesson depends as much on having the pupils with you as on simply supplying the materials. When children want to learn and develop their understanding they will use the teacher as a resource rather than an oracle. They will feel free to question, to suggest, and to give information, and this is what Mrs Adamant found so surprising. These pupils may have learned more about relationships from Mrs Adamant's reponse than they ever could from a book or an exercise.

Question 2
One of the problems with classroom authority lies in its very nature. Unless used with care it can easily distance a teacher from her pupils. The line between authority and authoritarianism is crossed only too easily if you are anxious to avoid indiscipline. Mrs Adamant's pupils were beginning to learn something of the range of human behaviour across all levels. What was so important to them was that the replies came from somebody that they may previously have considered as having no human side at all. When Mrs Adamant moved to the front of her desk she signalled a more relaxed and intimate discussion. She gave the pupils a covert signal that it was acceptable to ask questions of a more searching and even personal nature.

Question 3
Confidence is one area that is clearly reflected in nonverbal communication. Having moved to the front of her desk, Mrs Adamant was far more likely to have involved the group through the use of arm, hand, and facial gesture. Her posture would have been less defensive, her gestures would have emphasised and underlined certain points. Her enthusiasm would have been reflected in her face through eye contact and open smiling. All these nonverbal indicators would have signalled clearly to the pupils Mrs Adamant's enjoyment and enthusiasm for the discussion and her new-found confidence with the class.

Question 4   If we accept that many of Mrs Adamant's pupils would have known of her usual teaching style, either by reputation or by direct experience, then we can begin to understand why Mrs Adamant's early stance had such an impact on the class. They may previously have regarded her as distant, cold, a practitioner who was only interested in facts. They would have been wary if her reputation was of control maintained by an ever-increasing series of threats and authority dictated by red pen. Now Mrs Adamant found herself able to show that she could confidently maintain her control whilst dealing with their questions and their reactions in a flexible and sympathetic way. Mrs Adamant could capitalise on this in the future in a number of ways. She could begin to use active sessions, where the pupils worked together in groups, reporting back and involving her in the subsequent discussion. These techniques could also be transferred to her subject teaching, allowing for a free exchange of ideas within a more positive and mutually supportive atmosphere. This may all sound a little far-fetched – too much to expect, perhaps — but such changes can be observed in people who learn to display enthusiasm. Think of your own closest friends; is it not the case that much of your pleasure in being with them is the positive and enthusiastic way in which they respond to you?

Chapter 8

Confrontations; or, the Empire Strikes Back

Dealing with confrontations is perhaps the most difficult task in the eyes of an inexperienced teacher; and no teacher, no matter how experienced, can avoid confrontations for very long. Our aims in the chapters so far have been to show how you can avoid unnecessary confrontations by engaging the children's interest and attention, and how potential trouble-makers can be recognised. When confrontations do occur, they can present you with a major problem, because handling them successfully requires skills which are seldom exercised in normal social life.

In adults most mild confrontations - at least between relative strangers in a public place, which is the equivalent of the classroom situation - are dealt with verbally, and the demands of politeness require that they do not really come out into the open. Usually one party gives way at an early stage. Privately the opponents may have extremely strong views on the matter, but they are either suppressed, or are expressed in an oblique and rational way. In such confrontations, disagreements are seldom carried to outright rejection of the other's point of view. Most overt confrontations between adults involve people of approximately equal status (e.g. two motorists arguing after a car accident), rather than one person asserting authority over another; so as a new teacher you are likely to lack experience in the skills of ordering people about!

Nor can you base your technique on the children's conflict behaviour. In the last resort their arguments are settled by fighting (Neill 1991a). Especially in early adolescence, playful rough-and-tumble among boys and verbal insult among girls may be conspicuous as children bargain for status and friendship. Although you need to be able to communicate with the children in terms they understand, you cannot use these tactics. Older boys, for example, may be quite happy to accept horseplay from their friends while rejecting it from you. Satisfactory reaction to a challenge from the class requires an understanding of dominance and the way it is expressed behaviourally.

DOMINANT DOES NOT MEAN DOMINEERING

You need first to distinguish between dominance and threat; confusion between these two is at the root of many of the problems that inexperienced teachers encounter. *Dominance* is the ability to control or influence the behaviour of others. *Threat* is behaviour which indicates that there is a risk of physical attack or sanctions (i.e. an escalated confrontation) unless the opponent gives way, though mild threat (as illustrated in Chapter 6) indicates the risk is not imminent. Dominance does *not* imply a confrontation; in fact if dominance is well-established, the subordinate will give way without any confrontation. Threat indicates that dominance is not fully established, and the more extreme the threat, the greater the risk to dominance (Figure 8.1).

Figure 8.1 An angry teacher. A more confident person would advance, rather than showing strong intention movements of attack (the forward bend) without moving. Many children saw this teacher as 'angry or upset'; a few saw her as 'strict'

There are two implications of this for the new teacher. Firstly, dominants behave in characteristic ways; if you behave like a dominant, you are likely to be treated as one. Children devote a lot of time to learning social skills and rules, and if you can play by these rules you will be an effective operator. You must behave as a dominant when you are not being challenged as well as when you are. This is the 'getting attention' behaviour we described in Chapter 6. Secondly, you must manipulate the classroom interaction so that, as far as possible, disputes are on unimportant issues where it pays neither party to threaten a serious confrontation. This will often mean dealing with a problem at an early stage; once either party has committed themselves and stands to lose face, a dispute is no longer 'unimportant'. If you can establish dominance at a low level you will be at an advantage in any future more serious dispute which cannot be avoided.

WHAT EFFECTIVE TEACHERS DID

When we looked at effective teachers' behaviour during confrontations in the video study, we found that their behaviour was both more decisive and more relaxed than that of ineffective teachers. Obviously there is a problem in deciding exactly when a confrontation begins and ends; we took the easy way out, and looked only at what the teacher was doing during actual critical talk. Firstly, effective teachers behaved in a more decisive way; they used more controlling gestures, such as baton forward (Figure 6.12) and fend (Figure 7.3). The child sees a teacher who knows her own mind and is in control. Secondly, the effective teachers were more animated; they used more illustrative gestures (Figure 7.11), in particular the 'imitative gestures' which signal especially vividly what the teacher is talking about (Figure 7.12), and they used animated intonation more, showing a lively and often humorous involvement in what they were saying. This indicates a teacher who was forceful but neither unduly angry nor sarcastic. On the other hand, they used a loud voice less than other teachers – shouting is threatening. (We did not see actual physical attacks often enough for them to show up in the statistical analysis, but the effective teachers never attacked children, though some other researchers (e.g. Beynon 1985) have seen effective teachers using physical violence.)

Overall, the effective teachers were more self-confident and decisive. This picture fits previous work, for example the important studies of Kounin (1970) on discipline. Kounin found that what he called 'withitness' had stronger correlations with work involvement and low deviancy than any other aspect of teachers' behaviour in first and second-grade primary classrooms. 'Withit' teachers chose the right child as the target for their disciplinary actions – they did not pick on a child who had joined an already misbehaving group while ignoring the instigators, or correct a child for a minor offence such as whispering to a neighbour while other children were engaged in something more serious such as throwing things around the room; and they reacted at the right time, intervening as soon as deviancy started, rather than letting it run on and build up.

This gives the impression that the effective teachers were dour martinets, but that would be misleading – in other work we found 'strict' teachers were disliked. In fact the effective teachers tempered their control by using more prosocial behaviour (including smiling, getting down to the child's level and so on – Figure 8.2) to defuse conflicts, and they were more relaxed – for example, they were more likely to stand with their hands in their pockets.

What a smile means during a confrontation depends on its exact context. We normally think of smiling as indicating pleasure and friendliness, but the pleasure can be at someone else's expense and the friendliness can have an ingratiating quality. In the charged atmosphere of a confrontation these subtleties of meaning can take on considerable significance. If you smile while actually criticising a child it suggests to the

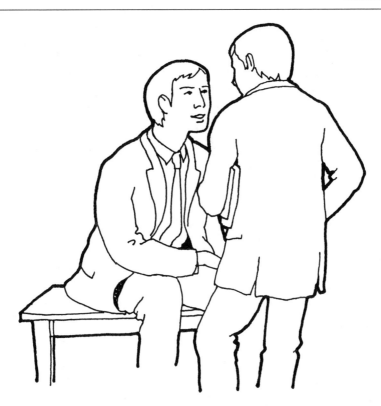

Figure 8.2 Drawn from a confrontation in which the teacher was reasoning with the child, which the teacher won. The critical features are the more relaxed posture of the teacher (particularly his facial expression and the fact that he sat on the desk): the boy, despite his casual posture, remained absolutely still while being talked to. Children who saw this picture without knowing the background interpreted the teacher as 'helpful', 'friendly' and 'easy going', confirming the indications from our videotape study that effective teachers used positive non-verbal signals to defuse the effect of verbal criticism

child that you are actually enjoying the confrontation and are in no doubt of winning; it also has a mocking quality. When a child smiles while you are criticising him and answers back this is a serious sign that your authority is at risk; again the smile is the mark of the winner (Figure 8.3). An important point here is that a smile given while *failing* to meet a challenge has quite a different meaning. Under these circumstances smiling is a submissive gesture, the mark of a loser. By smiling at a misdemeanour and failing to take any other action you are signalling both that the children can take the initiative and (because the children are more aware of the social than the submissive meaning of the smile) you will seem to be amused by or actually approve of it – whatever your conscious feelings. Hence the well-worn 'Don't smile till Christmas'. This impression will be reinforced if you show some other patterns typical of our ineffective teachers; barrier signals (Figure 6.5) or fumbling and other 'displacement' actions (Figure 6.6). We discussed the significance of these in Chapter 6; in our observations they appeared as clear signals to the class that the teacher was uncertain

Figure 8.3   The boy's posture is more relaxed than the teacher's hands-on-hips; his clothing and smile also indicate clearly that he does not take her threats seriously. Drawn from a confrontation in which the boy moved around, and looked out of the window while the teacher was trying to reason with him; the teacher lost. Smiling does not always indicate defiance: if the child smiles while in a submissive posture, it is an appeasing gesture

how to deal with the confrontation and that her attitude was defensive rather than self-confident. We also found the ineffective teachers were more likely to have a sad expression during a confrontation; there could be no clearer signal to the class that the teacher was worried that she could not cope.

Knowing the sanctions available

First, you must rule out physical force as a sanction. The problem is that you cannot use the amount of force which would cow the children into submission. When you see red, you might dearly love to pull out your pearl-handled revolver and plug Albert between the eyes. Certainly a miraculous calm would descend for the rest of the lesson as you stood over Albert, your gun smoking in your hand. Unfortunately for this lovely vision, not only is capital punishment illegal, but any other form of assault (Figures 8.4 and 8.5) could have led to legal action (Partington 1984), even before the recent legal change outlawing corporal punishment. Quite apart from the legal aspect, any form of physical attack which does not completely disable the opponent runs the risk of possible physical counter-attack; Humphries' study (1981) of children at the beginning of this century describes their fierce and sometimes successful resistance to the severe corporal punishment used by teachers at that time. If you use force and there is any resistance, you will find yourself engaged in a tussle, and dominants do not engage in tussles. Resistance is very likely; two questionnaire studies (Neill 1991a) have shown that children dislike attacks, and see them as an indicator of the 'over-strict' teacher, their most unpopular type.

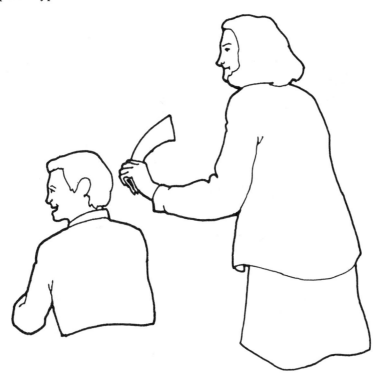

Figure 8.4 Swatting a child, one of a range of unofficial physical attacks. Children agreed this teacher was 'strict' or 'angry'

There is therefore every likelihood that physical force will merely stir up resistance, even if it does not lead to complaints to parents or senior staff. *This makes it essential that you do not get provoked into losing your temper and lashing out as a result.* This is a particular risk for idealistic teachers who care for their subject and the children. When you really want the children to learn and they play you up, you may find this so downright irritating and be so hurt at this opposition to what you believe in that your reaction is explosive. Professional detachment is vital here, however difficult; you must stick to 'conventional' tactics. Chief among these conventional tactics is a knowledge of the sanctions built into the school system, especially school rules and the support of the hierarchy.

If you are to use the rules and the hierarchy effectively, you must have a thorough knowledge of the back-up available before you need to make use of it. Dominants act

Figure 8.5 Quelling a child. Any use of brute force is likely to be resented. Children saw this teacher as 'strict', 'angry' and 'unfriendly'

fast and decisively; in a crisis you must act at once and your reaction must be correct. Even uncertainty or muddle with equipment, such as a slide projector, can be enough to get a giggle from the class and can begin to unsettle order – a strong reason for good preparation.

You must have familiarised yourself with the rules that the school or your department has to cover particular situations. Are the class supposed to line up before the lesson in the playground or outside the classroom door, or can they come straight in? Should they stand until you give them permission to sit at the start of the lesson, or to dismiss at the end? Should they stand up if a visitor enters the room? Do they need permission from you before they can take their jackets off? What is the procedure if a child loses a book – where can he get a new book, and what does it cost? If you show ignorance and indecisiveness on these points, you will immediately have a credibility problem. This presupposes, of course, that the hierarchy will support you effectively – for instance by calling in parents, who can apply the sanctions which you are legally forbidden to use. If senior staff fail in their duty to support you when a situation moves beyond the sanctions you are allowed to use, the school is likely to have severe discipline problems because its pupils will have learnt they can get away with anything; but this is hardly your responsibility.

A CONFRONTATION ACCORDING TO THE RULES

Rules, whether they are imposed from outside or you formulate them specifically for your own classroom, can be used to depersonalise confrontations between child and teacher. Effective teachers present rules as something above both teacher and child, which both have to obey, or as a bargain which both have to keep to. The situation ceases to be defined as a confrontation between teacher and child, which the child might be able to win or negotiate his way out of; you now appear to be as much bound by the terms of the rules as the child (Torode 1976). If you discipline him it becomes joint obedience rather than personal malice. Sometimes you may wish to present yourself as a friendly and sympathetic character by 'colluding' to bend the rules. It is important to note here that the rules are still defined as being in force; this is not the same as colluding to break them. Rogers (1991) develops this approach with extensive practical examples; he feels that as automatic respect for authority decreases, teachers have to establish mutual respect with their classes through a framework of rules.

A nice example of this use of rules, illustrating several other points as well, comes from the Geography teacher, Mr Weathering, whom we have referred to before. It is his third lesson with the class; he is checking on whether homework has been done. He knows that at least one boy has failed to do so, because he came to tell him so quietly as the class entered, but was told to sit down because Mr Weathering wants to make the point publicly. Two boys have to stand up because they did not do the homework; one has been dismissed with a valid excuse – he was knocked down by a seven-tonne lorry the previous week. By dealing with this boy sympathetically but humorously, Mr Weathering establishes his human side; but making the boys stand up isolates them in front of their peers and establishes his control. This leaves the boy who talked to him privately.

Mr Weathering [advancing down towards the second boy, with an expression of pleased surprise (Figure 8.6)]:   Now we come to the last gentleman. [*Stopping, and regarding the boy (Figure 8.7); speaking quietly.*] What are you going to tell me?
Boy [Almost inaudible]:   Left it at home, sir.
Mr Weathering: Pardon?
Boy: Left it at home, sir.
Mr Weathering [advancing]:   **Now**, if I remember, . . . when we started at the beginning of term, we made a **contract** with each other [Figure 8.8]. I said *I* would set homework **once a fortnight** [*with air purse, Figure 7.17*], in big dollops, to give you plenty of time to do it, so that I could collect it at the next lesson, didn't I?
Boy [Almost inaudibly]:   Yes, sir.
Mr Weathering: Now if you break **your** half of the bargain with **me** [Figure 8.9], what would be a fair return for that? [*Silence*] Well?
Boy: Bring it in on Monday, sir.

Figure 8.6   This is a modification of the chin-up 'plus face' (Figure 6.3); the more extreme brow-raise and smile indicate pleased surprise. The expression indicates, at the start of the confrontation, that it is going to be an unexpected pleasure

Mr Weathering: No it wouldn't [*class giggles*]; we're misunderstanding each other. I'll tell you what the contract is. **You** bring your book in on time [Figure 8.10], and *I* set work once a fortnight in big dollops [*grinning and stabbing down into his palm*]. But if you **forget** – I break **my** part of the bargain, and you get **two** big dollops **once a week!** [Figure 8.11] [*Class giggles*] And that is a rotten deal, isn't it? [*Class giggles.*] Do you think I'm joking? [Figure 8.12.] [*Silence.*] Do you?
Boy: No sir.
Mr Weathering: No I'm not. You're going to discover tonight that I'm not joking [*grinning smugly*] you're going to be the **only** one this week with an extra dollop [*class giggles*] [Figure 8.13]. [*Briskly*] Sit yourself down. [*Turning, and as he walks to the front:*] Now boys, no talking for the next few minutes. What I want you to do is put up that heading. . . .

A minute later, another boy asks: Is that a felt-tip, sir? (There is a box on Mr Weathering's desk, but there is a school rule against felt-tip pens.)

Figure 8.7 The use of eyes side (Figure 9.2) with head cant dramatises Mr Weathering's close attention on the boy as he waits for an answer, increasing the pressure on him

Mr Weathering [in a voice of incredulity; involvement with the boy asking the question is indicated by his forward lean, and gaze]: Now that's a **sinful word**, isn't it? *[showing dominance by a 'forward baton' [Figure 6.11] with his finger, and a teasing attitude by the smile and raised eyebrows]* Felt-tips? *[Taking one from the box]* Those are **fibre**-tips. That's not even a tip, is it? *[Class laughs; he takes another.]* Those are fibre-tips.
Boy: Oh.
Mr Weathering: If anybody asks you what you use in Mr Weathering's lesson . . .
Boy: Fibre-tips.
Mr Weathering: Fibre-tips, that's right. If they're felt-tips, then you use fibre-tips.
Boy: Can I have a red fibre-tip?
Mr Weathering: Fibre-tip. Yes.

In this incident Mr Weathering did four things. He defined the failure to hand work in as an infraction of a rule (which had in fact been stated, without much ceremony, in answer to a boy's query about homework at the start of the first lesson with this class). Secondly, he made the experience uncomfortable for the boy by his use of silence and questions, throwing the boy on to the defensive; his non-verbal style indicated that he was calm, expected no serious challenge, and was enjoying the experience. So far, this implies that the confrontation was a completely stress-free experience for him; but, as we characteristically found, effective teachers usually showed 'displacement' behaviour before or after a confrontation or transition between activities (when the temporary lack of focus again produces the risk of disorder). In this case he had been showing

Figure 8.8 The upward baton carries an aggressive message, as it is a ritualised and miniature version of the downward beat (Figure 8.4), the primitive human aggressive movement. It therefore adds force to the accompanying words

barrier signals and intention escape movements (see Chapter 6) as he prepared to ask the class about their homework, but, characteristically of effective teachers, the 'line went clear' as he actually launched into the interrogation. The class were not attending closely during the waiting period; they began to monitor him as the confrontation started, when he was no longer showing the evidence of uncertainty. Thirdly, he made a smart transition into the business of the lesson, without wasting time on the transition (Kounin 1970). Fourthly, the incident of the fibre-tips showed that, as a senior member of staff, he could humorously collude to modify the school rules – which he was largely responsible for setting up. He thus demonstrated that he could be 'one of the lads' as well as an inexorable authority.

The follow-up to this incident is also worth noting. Mr Weathering gave the boy who had left his book at home the paper he needed to do his classwork, without further comment. At the end of the lesson he called the boy to the front, and put an avuncular arm over his shoulder (which made the boy squirm horribly) (Figure 8.14). He then showed the boy the extra work he would have to do; but allowed him, if he promised to be very good, to be let off this time, and to bring his homework in on Monday (as the boy had originally suggested). Immediately afterwards, as the class went out, Mr Weathering noticed a pile of pencil shavings on the desk; calling the boy's name with an expression of astonishment, he told him to 'sweep them up into a big hand, and put them in the bin'. Having asserted the rule-bound order of his classroom, making the

Figure 8.9 Self-pointing is used in a variety of situations to reinforce the view one holds. Here it emphasises Mr Weathering's part in the 'bargain' he is describing

Figure 8.10 A modified use of the forceful air chop or punch (Figure 7.11) Mr Weathering is almost hammering on the rule-book (which does not actually exist) which the boy should have been attending to

Figure 8.11 Counting off the two pieces of work a fortnight. The smile again indicates (like that in Figure 8.6) Mr Weathering's confidence in what he is doing, and willingness to impose the punishment

Figure 8.12 A continuation of the previous gesture, but the emphasis has now switched to checking that the message has been received; this is signalled by the eyes side (compare Figure 8.7)

Figure 8.13 Posture is now more relaxed, reflecting pleasure that the message has got home

boy thoroughly uncomfortable in front of his peers, Mr Weathering did not harbour a grudge. Many teachers would have exploded at the minor indiscipline and sloppiness represented by the shavings, leaving the boy in a state of festering ill-feeling. Overall, his approach was particularly suited to a formal school environment, but even with this level of disciplinary skill, he experienced mucking about and poor work later in the school year!

If a rule is to be presented effectively in this way, you must appear to be bound by it consistently; homework must, for instance, be required on every occasion. A lengthy discussion should not happen every time; it rapidly loses its impact, and the lesson can be used more productively. On future occasions a briefer restatement of the rules should suffice.

Showing up

The confrontation we have just described is an example of 'showing up' (Woods 1975). In the hands of a skilled practitioner, this can be a technique of deadly effectiveness. Showing up involves a reprimand intended to embarrass a child in front of his peer group; this can be one of the most effective punishments you can use. As Woods has indicated, there can be both practical and moral objections to its use. Many teachers may have moral scruples against a calculated attempt to embarrass a child (though, as Woods points out, showing up sometimes happens accidentally, when a teacher is unaware of what hurts a child's feelings). On a practical level, many children have

Figure 8.14 Apparently friendly contact used as a punishment; this level of familiarity is inappropriate for a teaching situation, and therefore constitutes 'showing up'. It indicates a high level of dominance by the teacher; with a less dominant teacher the boy would have been able to object, and the move would have been counter-productive

considerable skills of repartee, and the inexperienced teacher may find herself hoist with her own petard. In addition, the potential of the technique is dangerously seductive, and after initial successes there is a risk that you may become hooked on a policy of wounding sarcasm, which keeps the class under grumbling control at the cost of alienation. Wragg and Wood's (1984) 'Mr Baker' exemplifies this style, and we also encountered it in our study.

However, provided showing up is not used in a vindictive way and you make a positive approach to make clear that you can show social approval as well as social disapproval, showing up has much to recommend it. It provides instantaneous punishment, and may be less disruptive than more overt forms of confrontation. This example comes from the first Music lesson of the year; Mr Rhythm has had to improvise because the music rooms are being redecorated, so he cannot use the instruments. As one of a range of activities, the class have been singing 'My Bonny Lives over the Ocean', standing up or sitting down each time they came to a B. At the end of the song:

Mr Rhythm: That's very clever Albert; we'll be coming to that in a moment.
Albert: What?
Mr Rhythm [miming it]:   Standing up and sitting down the opposite way to everybody else. [*The class giggles; Albert says nothing.*]

Albert is in a difficult position. What can he do? Overtly he has been praised. He can hardly reject the praise, for instance by saying 'No, it isn't!' To do so would be to escalate from his, at the moment, ambiguous challenge (if asked, he might have claimed that he wasn't very good at keeping time) to an unequivocal one; and he knew, and knew that Mr Rhythm knew, that he was trying to be clever in the first place. An unequivocal challenge is not a risk he would want to take at this early stage in his knowledge of Mr Rhythm. He cannot say 'I'm so glad you noticed'. Nor can he blush, and say 'It was nothing really'. Either, if taken literally, would label him as a creep, though if he knew Mr Rhythm to be harmless, he could turn either of these responses into an open challenge by using a suitably poncy tone of voice. His correct response would be along the lines of, 'I'm afraid I can't accept the implied meaning of your statement', but he is hardly likely to think that one up on the spur of the moment.

This example also suggests that effective showing up may be the prerogative of the experienced teacher. If Mr Rhythm has taught this lesson before, he will already have encountered just this situation. His shot is waiting, ready to be fired; he only requires the appropriate target. The unfortunate Albert has not encountered this ambush before and therefore has to think on his feet. If you were a new teacher in Mr Rhythm's position you might not have thought of this situation arising; or you might not have thought it necessary to have a riposte primed and ready.

Showing up in this way, like many other aspects of discipline, is easier for the experienced teacher, simply because she knows what to expect. However, the technique can be used extremely successfully by inexperienced teachers. For example, Mr Imagery, a student teacher of English, working for the first time with a secondary class, threatened jovially that those who produced the worst pieces of work on *Animal Farm* would have to sing the 'Animals' Song' from the book, in front of the whole class, at the end of his set of lessons. This threat was effective as much because of the pleasurable anticipation with which it was delivered, as because of the potential embarrassment which the sanction would cause. In fact one potential member of the choir skipped the last lesson, in order to save her blushes, which suggests the threat was rather excessive. The rest, however, took part in a caterwauling chorus, with Mr Imagery joining in; as he said, this was only fair. This makes an important point about the satisfactory use of showing up, which the three teachers we have discussed illustrate. All were generally supportive, offering the class positive rewards as well as the very negative reinforcement of showing up. They all behaved in a humorous way, and were ready to joke with pupils. Their showing up, therefore, merged into the type of playful ribbing which is characteristic of informal social groups. Their classes were like such groups in their surface structure of friendly chat, which softened the control which they exerted over their lessons.

To conclude, it is important to stress that showing up can have a positive value, but the way in which it is presented is critical. In such situations children are extremely sensitive to non-verbal nuances which suggest whether your underlying approach is teasing or hostile. If showing up is done in a wounding way, with no compensation in support and praise for the children, they will find the classroom a hostile environment and reject you, the subject, or both. If the children are free to reciprocate on an equal footing, you have lost control.

Withdrawing to a one-to-one confrontation

Straight criticism of children's conduct or work, and overt anger, also have a place in classroom management; you must be able to show anger in situations which genuinely require it. However, occasions requiring anger should be rare, and calm but relentless firmness is the best aim. You must be prepared to escalate firmly at an early stage in initial encounters, before things have got out of hand. Once control has been established, you can afford to ignore closed challenges. However, if you meet a serious open challenge at any stage, you must face it, and often this is best done on a one-to-one basis, so that the child does not have the support of his peers, and you do not have to perform in front of a potentially hostile audience. No audience means a lower risk of social humiliation, and therefore reduces the severity of the challenge for both sides. One-to-one confrontations are closer to the inexperienced teacher's general social experience and to be preferred for this reason as well. We deal with this and other aspects of one-to-one interaction in the next chapter.

SUMMARY

Threat signals indicate the risk of overt conflict, and must be separated from dominant signals which indicate the ability to control the behaviour of others without conflict. Excessive threat is likely to be counter-productive. Dominant teachers exert calm, decisive control, using rules to depersonalise conflicts, and friendly relationships to make conformity rewarding. Careful observation of experienced teachers is necessary to detect the non-verbal signals used, which are less obvious than threatening signals. Exerting social pressure through 'showing up' can also be highly effective, but needs highly developed social skills to be done without excessively offending the pupil. Dealing with a confrontation in privacy allows you to use your normal social skills, and deprives the disruptive pupil of an audience.

The training materials deal with the problem of assessing a challenge in context and picking the most appropriate counter-measure.

TRAINING MATERIALS

There are times in our lives when we cannot avoid confrontation. It is part, albeit an unpleasant part, of the dynamics of communication; indeed, it seems to be an almost essential ingredient in political communication! In a classroom, however, things are very different and the stakes somewhat more immediate.

Confrontations are relatively rare in the Sixth Form, where reasoned and rational solutions can be found, often after eloquent and articulate debate. Year nine on a Friday afternoon, however, may require an altogether different technique.

Pictorial exercise – 'Don't do as I do, do as I say!'

Dominance is the important ingredient in avoiding confrontation, or at least in controlling and neutralising it before it becomes a threat to your authority.

Question 1   Take the image shown in Figure 8.15. Here we have a light-hearted scene of three pupils intent on enjoying themselves. The challenge seems largely closed in nature, but you have asked the class to finish their written work quietly. Clearly not everyone is listening.

Now look at the images shown in Figures 8.16–8.19, drawn from videotapes of dominant, effective teachers.

Which do you feel would be most effective in approaching this situation, and why? Which approaches, if any, are likely to be antagonistic? Assuming you had told the group to 'stop talking' on several previous occasions, would that change your opinion as to the most appropriate approach?

Figure 8.15

Figure 8.16

Figure 8.17

Figure 8.18

Figure 8.19

Descriptive Exercise – Don't do as I do!

In the early days of teaching, many new teachers get their experience and ideas for classroom discipline from their older and more practised colleagues. Much of this advice is useful; some, however, is not only misguided, but, used by an inexperienced member of staff, can prove disastrous. In the following example, Ms Tyro, a young teacher, has been given some advice as to how she should deal with discipline and confrontations.

She has been told that in order to hold her own in the classroom she should stick to the following rules:

1 Set out the ground rules from the first lesson.
2 Make sure that the first pupil to break the rules is dealt with severely, thus setting an example to the others.
3 Do not be too friendly.
4 Do not accept any excuses.
5 Show them at the outset who is boss!

Armed with this 'advice' Ms Tyro entered the classroom, carrying her prep book firmly under her arm. She stood squarely behind the desk and introduced herself to the new class. She spoke to the back of the room, and at no point did she smile or give any indication of sympathy. She then sat at the desk, placing her file in front of her and proceeded to list her particular set of rules.

At one point during her introduction two pupils exchanged a brief comment regarding the time. She immediately stood, walked directly to them and, leaning towards them, shouted her disapproval, culminating in a threat to place the offenders in detention should they repeat their performance.

She taught the remainder of this first lesson in an atmosphere of virtual silence, the pupils mechanically performing their respective tasks.

Safe in her belief that her sound advice had led to a situation of perfect control she approached the lesson one week later. On this occasion, however, one pupil, Simon, who had been absent in the first week, returned; he had not had the benefit of her earlier performance. He sat quietly to begin with, but seemed to become increasingly noisy and agitated as the lesson progressed, particularly when Ms Tyro again admonished two pupils for the offence of rocking on their chairs.

Simon soon lost interest in the lesson and began to dismantle his pen, eventually sending the pieces flying across the room. Ms Tyro, acting on her earlier advice, gave him a severe and public rebuke, ordering him to pick up the pieces and throw them in the bin. Simon refused, saying that it was 'his pen and he could fix it'.

The other pupils quickly stopped their work and silence fell as they watched the confrontation develop. Ms Tyro, aware that her authority could be on the line, rapidly moved towards Simon shaking her index finger and shouting. She made it clear that 'I will not tolerate this behaviour. You will stay behind after the lesson'. Before Simon could reply she turned sharply and, walking back to her desk, picked up the pieces of the pen and threw them in the bin.

Simon reacted instantly to this move. 'You can't do that,' he shouted, 'that's my pen'. He got up from the desk, walked to the bin and took out the pieces of his pen. He then looked directly at Ms Tyro, saying, 'I've had enough of you, I'm going' and moved to leave the room. Ms Tyro stood in his way shouting at him to sit down.

Question 1   Was Ms Tyro's initial advice sound or misguided, and was she right to act on it in the way she did?

Question 2   Why did the class react as they did in the first few lessons? What signals was Ms Tyro sending out by the stance that she chose to take?

Question 3   Is there a point where you feel that Ms Tyro made an error of judgement, and did her subsequent actions reinforce that error?

Question 4   How much difference do you think it made that Simon missed the first lesson? What differences would there have been in the signals Ms Tyro sent in the first lesson and in her subsequent lesson?

Question 5   How do you feel Ms Tyro should deal with the situation at the end? What long and short-term strategies can she adopt to assist her in recovering the situation and regaining the balance of power, both in relation to Simon and to the remainder of the class?

TRAINING MATERIALS – ANSWERS TO EXERCISES

Figure 8.15 To choose which is likely to be the best approach to this group it is worth drawing a few conclusions as to what may be happening. It may be that they are discussing the task at hand – at least that is what they will probably tell you – but you have asked them to finish their written work, so this is a challenge to your authority. The two talking girls present a closed challenge as their activities are neither disguised nor involving peripheral pupils. The third seems temporarily absent from the real world, although she may be thinking task-oriented thoughts!

The most effective approach will relate, at least to some extent, to what you characteristically use in classroom situations. In this respect our interpretations may not fit precisely with yours, but they should give an insight as to how each signal is likely to be interpreted.

Figure 8.16 The forward lean is an intention movement of approach, while the desk acts as a barrier between teacher and class. This could be an effective approach to Figure 8.15, but it would depend to some extent on the physical distance between teacher and pupils, and their relationship. Almost all children saw this teacher as 'friendly' or 'easy-going' because of her smile, but the lean indicates that she is quietly reinforcing her presence. The same posture with a frowning expression was seen as much stricter. Where the relationship with the class is good, and with cooperative pupils, the smiling forward lean would be effective even at a distance. It would have more impact, but still without seeming hostile, if she approaches the group, standing by the pupils in the foreground. Her approach will attract their attention; a question – 'Any problems?', or the like – should re-engage all three, without any recriminations as to what they have been doing. Similar moves with a frown may have a more immediate effect, but may induce unnecessary resentment as a first move, since they convey a critical attitude. However, any resistance to the more friendly smiling approach should be met immediately by a perceptibly sharper response.

Figure 8.17 Hands in pockets, a relaxed posture. Many children saw this teacher as 'easy-going', in which case the stance would only be effective if her authority were not already challenged. Our material shows that this posture can be used very effectively by experienced teachers who have already established control; their calm questions, followed by silence waiting for a response, put trouble-makers 'on the spot', but still without any overtly expressed challenge. During first lessons, however, they were likely to use more assertive postures, such as hands on hips, or to respond immediately to any challenge, as for the lean and smile above.

Figure 8.18 Hands on hips is a threat posture; whilst it is still somewhat low key, it may be an effective way of reinforcing the message and showing that patience may be in short supply! Many children saw this as 'gets angry' or 'strict', partly due to the frowning expression. However the posture still conveys firmness when it is used with a neutral or even a smiling expression, and it is used very commonly by teachers. It can also be combined with other messages if only one hand is on the hip; if the other is in a pocket or is used to lean on something (Figure 6.2), the message conveyed is 'I'm calm about this but don't push your luck'.

Figure 8.19 Beckon; like the forward baton, this was seen as 'strict', 'angry', and 'unfriendly' and could be particularly effective if the low-key messages had not succeeded. A powerful command, the beckon indicates the assumed level of authority adopted by the user. Used appropriately it will reinforce authority within the classroom, but don't use it on the Headteacher in the staffroom, or you could fall from favour! Again, a smile makes the beckon rather less menacing, but it retains its message of power.

Descriptive exercise – Don't do as I do!

Question 1
Much of the advice given to Ms Tyro was far from sound: a mixture of cynicism and fear, couched in apparently justifiable terms. Some suggestions may have had a firm foundation, but, as with much staffroom folklore, their success is more a matter of individual personality than universal fact. Ms Tyro needed to be aware of what effect such advice would have on her relationship with the class if she followed all the points laid down for her. After all, each one was, in its own way, grossly authoritarian and gave no room for flexibility or for the development of positive classroom relationships. It was a charter for confrontation.

Question 2
It would be easy, if not glib, to say that the class reacted as if they were shell-shocked, but to some extent this would have been the effect. They were new to Ms Tyro, as she was to them. The first few days, sometimes known as the 'honeymoon period', are a time when pupils and teachers take the opportunity to look, listen, observe, and begin to draw conclusions as to the dynamics of their relationship. Ms Tyro's signals were quite clear. She would have been seen as aggressive, short tempered, somewhat apprehensive and certainly distant. She showed no signs of sympathy, preferring to invite confrontation rather than to seek empathy with the class. They would have felt that she chose to invade their personal space whilst creating and maintaining her own distance, and that she chose to see all events, even the most minor, as a personal challenge to her authority. If fear was her initial objective, then Ms Tyro succeeded in the first few days, but with the absence of any sort of working relationship with the class this single tactic was bound to fail when properly tested.

Question 3
There were several areas where Ms Tyro made mistakes. Her initial approach and her over-reaction to what were often low-level challenges would have done little to endear the children to her. Equally significant was the apparent lack of humour in her treatment of the pupils, which would also have reduced her standing in the popularity stakes. Her greatest misjudgement, however, was over the incident involving the pen. Many pupils have a clear view on what staff authority actions they regard as legitimate and within the acceptable range. Staff may take certain actions, touch or remove things (especially school equipment) without offending the classroom lawyers, but there are a number of definite 'no-go' areas. Some are so clear as to be understood mutually by

teachers and pupils – smacking or hitting, for example – but others can vary according to the pupil, class or even the school.

Ms Tyro's attitude to Simon was likely to cause confrontation, as she had not taken any opportunity to find out his reputation before their meeting and he, of course, had not had the benefit of the earlier 'introductory' lesson. Simon's dismantling of his pen presented only a closed challenge to Ms Tyro, as his actions did not seek to involve others. There was probably no real intent to disrupt the lesson, although clearly he was detached from the task in hand. An experienced teacher, confident and in control, would have taken steps to involve Simon in the lesson, or simply have given him time to settle to what was, after all, a new regime for both of them. Ms Tyro, however, appears to have judged this wrongly. Having seen Simon's behaviour as a serious challenge, her immediate tactic was to remove the offending object. The pen was not hers to remove, however (unlike a school book, ruler, calculator etc), unless, despite being private property, it was being used to create an open challenge. (For example, a sheath-knife would be an open challenge by its presence; but for a pen, Simon would have had to have done something like stabbing at a fellow-pupil, or squirting ink over his work.) Simon saw this as an illegitimate act, putting right very much on his side. Ms Tyro's action gave her little room to de-escalate the situation, but gave Simon the opportunity for a number of spectacular reactions.

Question 4

It is probable, with Ms Tyro's current level of skill, that if Simon had been present earlier, the same crisis would simply have occurred at an earlier stage. She had shown no signs of differentiating her treatment of the class as the week progressed, for instance by following up her initial demonstration of strictness by mellowing into sociability. If she had done so, the class could have been more sympathetic, as they would have seen Simon's behaviour as threatening a teacher whom they had come to like.

However, her strong reaction would have been seen as more legitimate if Simon's challenge had occurred early in the first lesson. At this stage, when teacher and class do not know each other, pupils are normally more cautious. This makes the same objective level of challenge more salient, and therefore more open. The class would have seen her fierce reaction to it as justified because the challenge would have created 'case law' as to how such incidents were to be dealt with in future. However, she would have needed to have used the tactics discussed below to defuse the situation somewhat, and it would have been better to deal with such a challenge by a very prompt, but lower-level reaction.

Question 5

The number of alternatives open to Ms Tyro at this stage is limited and none of them are guaranteed to be effective. In the eyes of the pupils, she has misused her authority and isolated herself from their support. By standing in front of Simon and placing a barrier between him and the door, she is inviting futher problems. One short-term strategy would be to let him go and to send a message, via a trusted member of the class, to a senior member of staff, briefly explaining the situation. Alternatively she could stand her ground and try to take the sting out of the situation by offering another pen and indicating that if he returns to his seat they will, together, restore his pen to its former glory at the end of the lesson. This could be a useful tactic if Ms Tyro is prepared to use it, as, although she may view it as a climb-down to some extent, it will show a measure of compassion and could be the first indication that she is prepared to negotiate, rather than dictate. This 'softening' of her approach seems essential at this stage, not only in terms of this situation, but to ensure the development of her relationship with the class as a whole. She cannot afford to harden her approach to the class any further; indeed, if she were to physically stop Simon, by holding him in some way, she could be sued for assault. In the long term her attitude to Simon and the remainder of this class will need careful consideration if she is to teach them effectively. She will need to ensure that her punishments are in proportion to the crimes and, just as importantly, that a crime has actually been committed in the first place!

An increase in gesture, facial and postural warmth, humour, and clear enthusiasm will all be needed if the class are to accept her. Ms Tyro clearly wants to succeed with this class and has gone to considerable lengths to create a climate which she felt would be conducive to a productive working relationship. What she may have failed to realise is that the productive relationship which she seeks will need to be two-way, and whilst it is essential that she remains in overall control, she must remain the source of the solutions, rather than the cause of the problems.

Chapter 9

Relationships with individual children

During periods when the children are working singly or in small groups, or at more informal times outside the class lesson period, you have a chance to talk to children individually, which can be invaluable in building up relationships with them. You may also be able to deal more productively with work or behaviour problems away from the attention of the whole class. On the other hand you may find the children take advantage of this, to become over-familiar or flirtatious. Excessive interest directed especially to deviations from the main course of the lesson suggests over-friendliness; as Denscombe (1980b) indicates, children may encourage you on social and friendly topics and try to change the subject as subtly as possible when you try to return to the work. This pattern can occur with teachers of either sex. We will return to the tactics to deal with it later.

Moving around the class when children are writing or engaged in practical work and talking to individuals is a situation much closer to the social situations with which you are familiar as an inexperienced teacher. It should therefore pose fewer problems than dealing with the whole class, because you can draw on your existing social skills. However, you need both to be able to behave in a way which makes clear your involvement with and interest in the children as individuals, and to react rapidly to any disturbance.

TALKING TO INDIVIDUALS IN THE CLASSROOM

All teachers go round and ask children about their work; the popular teacher indicates, by her behaviour as she goes round the class, that she is interested in the children first and their work second. As you move around, talking to children, you have a chance to show your appreciation of them as individuals. Children's feelings of social worth are very important to them, especially at secondary-school age; they are forced to make an assessment of their social worth in terms of school work on very limited evidence, simply because your attention has to be split between so many of them and you therefore have so little time for each individual. If a child not only receives very limited individual attention from you, as is inevitable, but when you are with him half your attention or more is taken away by distractions elsewhere in the class, he will decide that you have little interest in him as a person. He may well reciprocate by losing interest in you and what you have to offer. Though we have referred to the child as 'he' so far, this is especially a problem for girls, who are both more likely to be ignored because they are usually less obstreperous, and tend to feel your disregard more keenly (Stanworth 1983). It is obviously highly undesirable for girls to be ignored in this way, but research shows that teachers find it extraordinarily hard to distribute their attention evenly, despite efforts to do so. This is an even more likely problem if your control of the class is still tenuous, as you will be forced to give most attention to those who are more of a risk to your control. Once again, these are likely to be boys.

We have already mentioned, in Chapter 7, the ways in which you can show your attention and interest when children respond in a class session, and many of these signals are similar to those which are appropriate on a one-to-one basis. However, your closeness means that your signals to children come across as more intense than when you are standing eight or ten feet away in the whole-class situation, and you can therefore tone down the signals you give. For example, the extreme 'catching' posture shown in Figure 7.5 appears animated in a public context, but would be over the top if you were talking to a single child or a small group.

There are a range of signals used in normal social conversations which indicate attention to the companion; many of them appear in children's conversations. They are also appropriate for you to use when you are talking to children. In conversations, people orient their bodies towards each other and away from other people (see Exercises in Chapters 3 and 4); though, as we shall see, you cannot do this to the extent of losing awareness of other members of the class. Their gaze is on each other or the shared object of their attention (Ellis and Beattie 1986). If the child is the main speaker in a one-to-one classroom conversation (for example, if he is answering your questions) you should look at him for most of the time; otherwise he will think you are being inattentive. Equally, if you are explaining something, you should expect him to be watching your face, or the materials you are explaining, most of the time.

Listeners also show their attention to speakers by nodding (Ellis and Beattie 1986) or producing noises of attention such as 'ah-hum' as the speaker makes points, thus reassuring the speaker that her message has been taken in. This pattern refers to conversations between equals, where the speaker needs 'permission' from the listener to carry on, and will usually stop if lack of this feedback shows the listener is getting bored. When you are talking to children, their subordinate position means you need to give this feedback to 'permit' them to continue talking. At least initially, you would not expect to allow them to make this feedback to you, as they would then be controlling you! At this early stage, conversations should be one-sided – unless you are dealing with sixth-formers – with any feedback from the child showing respect rather than condescension. However, when the classroom relationship is well-established, genuine discussion between equals may be possible, with the children controlling the discussion as well as you.

To preserve the quality of individual dealings with your pupils, you must show what Kounin (1970) calls, with vivid but unlovely jargon, 'overlappingness', the ability to deal with an incident without losing track of what you were doing previously, as well as 'withitness', the ability to detect incidents in the first place through 'eyes in the back of your head'. 'Withitness' is perhaps even more important in this context than in the whole-class situations we dealt with in the last chapter. We examine these issues in more detail below, when we look at how you can deal with disruption elsewhere when you are talking to individuals, and how you can maintain vigilance by choosing an appropriate posture. First, however, we need to look at the type of signals you should definitely avoid giving.

How to look uneasy when children are working individually

Not only do inexperienced teachers who are rather unsure of themselves behave in a 'distant' way when talking to individual children, they usually move round the classroom in a defensive manner. Firstly they tend to walk incessantly, looking at children's books but seldom stopping to talk to them unless summoned. Patrolling among the 'hostile tribes' in this way gives the impression that you expect disorder, and can only cope with it by maintaining a state of constant readiness. Teachers who have a better relationship with their classes do not patrol them; they move from one child to another, usually taking the initiative in approaching children to see how they are progressing with their work. In this way they can check especially with children who are likely to need attention, for instance that low achievers have a satisfactory understanding of the lesson topic and are not being left behind. Even with high-achieving children it is important that you take the initiative in seeking out those with problems and dealing with them before they cause substantial difficulty, rather than waiting for them to reach a state of desperation and taking the initiative in calling for help. Thus Guy (1980) considered that many students who had been successful chemistry students in their school sixth forms were lost to the subject when they went to university, simply because they did not get the level of teacher involvement in chemistry practicals which they had received at school. The university demonstrators did not feel the same professional commitment to ensuring their charges benefited from the practicals as did schoolteachers.

Inexperienced teachers also show their defensiveness in their posture when they patrol the classroom; frequently they move around with their arms folded, with a hand on one hip, or with their hands in their pockets (Figure 9.1). As we saw in Chapter 6, these are mildly threatening postures. They are appropriate when you are facing the whole class and demanding their attention, but not when most children's attention is on their books and you are dealing with them in ones and twos. If you cannot face individual children without signs of getting rattled, you have problems. You should therefore try to avoid these postures if possible; even more so the body-cross postures

Figure 9.1 An ambivalent posture shown by a patrolling teacher; the body-cross indicates insecurity, the hand-on-hip is threatening. Children found it hard to assess this picture, giving both positive (e.g. 'helpful') and negative (e.g. 'boring') responses

and displacement activities discussed in Chapter 6, which are overt indicators of insecurity. If you are moving from child to child, as is preferable, with limited time in transit, you will have little time for these actions anyway, as you will be leaning on desks, dealing with books or materials, or pointing things out to children; but if you do have a distance to walk, you should let your hands hang by your sides in a relaxed way.

DISRUPTION DURING INDIVIDUAL WORK

The criteria for dealing with potential disruption when children are working individually are similar to those outlined in the previous chapter for incidents during whole-class teaching. In many ways your task is easier if incidents are isolated, because confrontations are less public in this situation. Much of the class will be aware neither of the incident nor of the fact that you are breaking off from your current task of teaching an individual, if they are involved in their own work. You must therefore ensure that your actions do nothing unnecessary to draw the attention of other children to the incident. Your best course is to stare towards the offending group if

Figure 9.2 Eyes side (left), usually held until the child reacts, signals 'I'm looking at you'. A brief eyes wide (right) and eyebrows flash also imply 'I'm surprised at you'. Children gave a mixture of positive reactions to both, such as 'friendly', 'fun', 'easy going' and 'calm'

their transgression and reputation is sufficiently mild (Figure 9.2). Otherwise you should use a close approach, lean over the children, and speak to them quietly.

Approaching to a close distance (Figure 9.3) intensifies the effect of any communica-

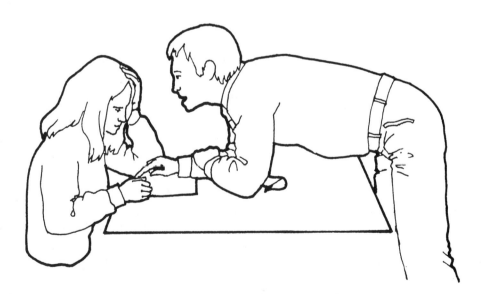

Figure 9.3 'Personal distance' between teacher and child. The meaning of the approach depends on the teacher's words and expression. Many children saw this teacher as helpful

tion between teacher and child. It also allows a very quiet voice – almost a whisper – to be used; the child is likely to reply spontaneously at the same volume (and can be told to keep his voice down if he does not). In this way a quite intense discussion can be held without children any distance away being aware of it. If you are criticising the child, you should remain standing and bend over him. You then imply dominance in three ways; your actual words are reinforced by your superior height, and your close approach indicates that you find the child no threat. Correcting a child while standing back from him is both less dominant and will involve talking at a greater volume, which is more likely to distract other children, so it should be avoided in most circumstances. However, with very argumentative children, especially in the fourth or fifth years, it may be better to stand back. Close approach is itself threatening (at the extreme there is a possibility of physical attack), and it may provoke a strong reaction.

CLOSE ENCOUNTERS OF THE TUTORIAL KIND

Close approach and a soft voice can also be used in a more positive way, as the best method for approaching children to talk about their work without disturbing others. With supportive talk and a friendly smile, this conveys interest in the child's problems and achievements. The close approach into the child's 'personal distance' (Hall 1966) intensifies the positive side of the interaction, provided you do not come too close, as we discuss below. Bending closely over children has two disadvantages, however. Firstly, it is more difficult for you to raise your head to look round if there is any sign of disturbance, especially behind you. You will need to straighten up in order to look round; this is both slower and more noticeable than glancing round from a standing position. Your surveillance over the class then seems to be more of an effort, and therefore more uncertain. 'Withitness', mentioned above, requires your surveillance to be unobtrusive but immediately accurate – it is difficult to be 'with it' when bending over. You may also not be 'with it' for a second reason. Few people are seen at their best from behind when bending over, and you may present a harmless (because you cannot see them) source of amusement to those members of the class presented with your rear view. A more upright standing posture, with less bend, largely solves these problems, but does not provide the desirable degree of intimacy in the talk between teacher and child. Sitting matches what would be done in friendly informal situations, but in most classrooms there are simply not the chairs available. Sitting on the desk or table, where there is room, has a more informal air, though it still leaves distance between you and the child – you are literally 'superior'. Kneeling beside the child (Figure 9.4) is probably the best solution. It allows you to get close, and as you come down to the child's level or below, you cease to dominate the child by your height. Kneeling is also seen as a 'humble' action, which would reinforce this. In addition, as your body axis is vertical, it is relatively easier to glance round behind yourself, maintaining your reputation for 'withitness'. As kneeling has so many advantages, it may be worth planning for this in advance by choosing clothes which will stand being knelt in.

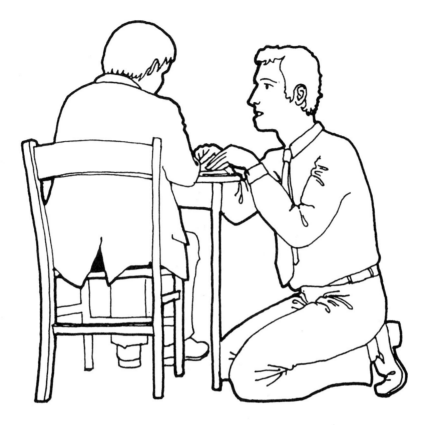

Figure 9.4 Kneeling, a sign of a teacher who is closely involved with the children. Almost all children saw this teacher as helpful; a few saw him as friendly

TOUCH

Close encounters with children on an individual basis may involve touch, which many teachers feel is a fraught area. Concern about child abuse has led to educational programmes designed to teach children to recognise and deal with unwelcome touches, (e.g. Baldwin and Lister 1987) and to concern among teachers that any touching may be interpreted as unprofessional conduct. Many authorities, such as Marland (1975) advise 'never touch a child in affection or anger'. What is permissible, and children's willingness to be touched, changes rapidly with age, which is a further problem if you are dealing with several age-groups. The permissible and inappropriate uses of touch can be understood by reference to its meanings. Outside the classroom, touch is an inevitable part of three types of interaction: nurturing (e.g. mother–baby or rescuer–injured person); aggression (e.g. fighting); and sexual. Milder forms of these three interaction types are touch used to convey affection, control, and flirtation (Figures 9.5 and 9.6).

Touch is such a valuable way of showing appreciation of children and concern for

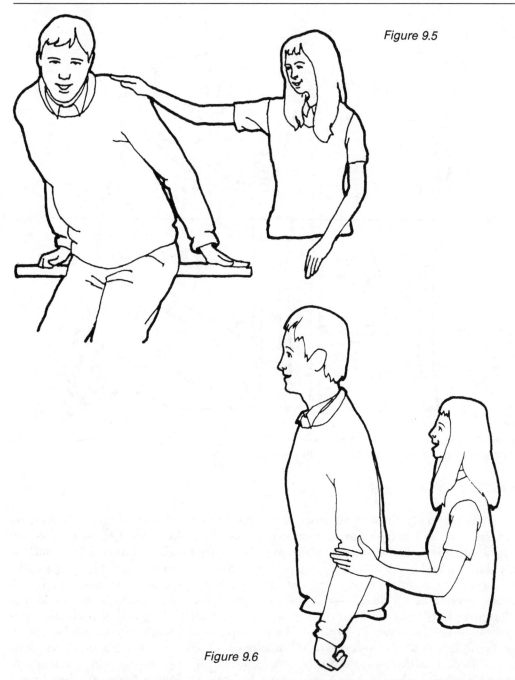

Figure 9.5

Figure 9.6

Figure 9.5, 9.6 Two successive incidents separated by about five seconds, during a practical lesson. The girl's approach was mildly flirtatious, but joking; the teacher moved rapidly out of reach at the touch at 9.5, but when he stopped, the girl touched him again (Figure 9.6), and he moved away again, with a humorous comment. Children described 9.5 as 'easy-going' or 'fun'

them, however, that it would be a pity if teachers felt compelled to avoid it altogether. Relatively few teachers touch even younger secondary-age children, though some individuals use touch quite extensively in these contexts, without apparent difficulty; it is of course much more frequent in the primary school, especially with infants. In classrooms at the younger end of the secondary age-range, and with top juniors, where there is a good relationship between teacher and class, supportive use of touch causes no problems where it arises naturally as part of the interaction, for instance when getting children's attention when they are moving around doing independent practical work, or moving or praising a child who is doing written work. Where the relationship between teacher and class is uncertain, or with older children, touch may be resented.

A study on the meaning of touch

We were particularly interested in the implications of touch because, while we saw relatively few examples of the friendly types of touch, they were seen very positively by children of the same age (Neill 1991a) – as positively as smiling, which is generally taken as a clear signal of friendliness. We therefore looked at touch in more detail with children aged eight to seventeen (Neill 1991b).

As might be expected, all groups of children disliked angry types of touch, such as being hit or having their head twisted round, reinforcing the point made elsewhere that teachers should not use this form of aggression against children. Rough-and-tumble (play-fighting touch) was also unpopular, though the older boys objected less than other groups. Some highly popular teachers, such as Ms Clemenceau described below, make effective use of it, but it is definitely to be avoided until you have built up a close relationship with the class. Rough-and-tumble is especially risky as children are likely to treat it as aggression if their relationship with you is distant. Directing touch does not raise the same objections; most of our groups would tolerate it. Most age-groups of boys appreciated friendly touch, though the girls were more equivocal, and comforting touch was appreciated by older children of both sexes.

Where these touches were directed was critical, however. The shoulder and arm were the most acceptable body areas to have touched, especially for the boys, and the chest and legs the least, especially for the older girls. This pattern was consistent across both sexes and all age-groups, though the differences were weaker in some cases than others. For instance, acceptance of friendly touch from teachers depended strongly on where it was received, but girls disliked angry touch from teachers to any part of the body; the college boys were happy with a friendly touch from a girl of their own age anywhere! Even with these extreme types of touch, the shoulders remained relatively acceptable, and the chest unacceptable. Back, head and hands were intermediate areas, but the head and hands, which are frequently touched by teachers of very young children, become less acceptable from eight or nine onwards, especially for girls.

You would be wise to restrict yourself to friendly and directing touch to the arm, shoulder and back; especially when you are new to the class, inappropriate use of touch can be potentially disastrous. For example, using apparently friendly touch as a punishment (Figure 8.14) can be a devastatingly effective 'showing up' tactic, but is too risky if your control is uncertain, as children will reject the touch indignantly.

We found that for most of the groups of children it made little difference, for touch in a public situation such as a classroom, whether the other person was a teacher or not – only the college-age boys strongly preferred a non-teacher. This fits with the general pattern, mentioned elsewhere, that children react to teachers in very much the same way as non-teachers. Familiarity and the sex of the other person were far more important. All children preferred a familiar person to an unfamiliar one, though the effect was weaker for the eight or nine-year-olds than the others. With age, children move from a preference for their own sex to one for the opposite sex. The eight or nine-year-old boys preferred to be touched by another male, but the older groups preferred females; this performance was very marked from twelve or thirteen on! The girls preferred to be touched by a female up to thirteen, and by an adult up to eleven. The fourteen or fifteen-year-old girls strongly preferred a male peer (though their tolerance for touch overall at this age was at its lowest), while by college age they did not discriminate strongly between the sexes, and with their increasingly adult status they made little distinction between adults and peers (this was also true of their male contemporaries).

From your point of view as a new teacher, these results underline a natural tendency for caution in touching members of a new class. There is also good reason, from the children's preferences, to be more cautious about touching older children than younger ones. (On the other hand, because touch is a generally more acceptable form of behaviour with younger children, it lacks with these age-groups the very powerful effects it can have on secondary children as a punishment (Figure 8.14), control or as a sign of friendliness.) Female teachers should perhaps be less reluctant to touch children than they often are; for most age-groups touch is likely to be more acceptable from them than from a male teacher. This applies to both sexes, the fourteen to fifteen-year-old girls being the most important exception.

Female teachers tend to be cautious of touching children, especially boys, because affectionate uses of touch may be misunderstood as having sexual implications and the touch might be reciprocated. However, it can be done with subtlety; a nice example recorded on one of our videotapes was the use of rough-and-tumble touch by Ms Clemenceau, a History teacher in a boys' school. Going round the room she noticed a boy who was doing his map wrong; she bent over, and took him by his tie. When he looked up, she produced a mock snarl and banged her forehead lightly but smartly against his before pointing out the error of his ways (Figure 4.5). She conveyed perfectly a combination of authority, cheerful playfulness and her relationship to the boy as a person, without any hint of 'come up and see me some time'. Not surprisingly, she was a very popular teacher, but you should be cautious in adopting this approach until you have established yourself with a class.

Depending on the individuals involved, a touch can convey two messages at once; thus the hands-on-shoulders posture done by a man to an attractive girl is frequently used in advertisements, conveying both dominance and sexual interest (Goffman 1979). Male teachers need to be aware of the obvious possibilities of misunderstanding if they use this touch. In general, the acceptability of nurturant touch decreases rapidly as children get older; the decrease is faster for children touching adults for reassurance (which, in the classroom context, has virtually dropped away to nothing by the time children leave the infant school) than for adults touching children. Controlling and dominant touch, which is frequent in primary schools (Evans 1979) also declines with age as children become less subordinate. The sexual implication of touch, of course, develops rapidly at puberty. The sum of these three patterns of development is that touch between children, as well as between children and adults, declines rapidly during the early years of secondary schooling. However, up to the third form, at least, children have not yet reached an adult touch status, and are likely to be more tolerant of, and even appreciative of, unambiguous forms of teacher touch. Since touch, like most non-verbal signals, offers itself to different interpretations, it can be used by older classes to signal an undesirable degree of over-familiarity.

Friendliness or flirtation?

One of the problems with touch, especially, and the other friendly one-to-one behaviours to a lesser extent, is that normal flirtation patterns include friendly actions. You need if possible to build up a friendly and cooperative relationship with your class, but to be able to react at once if things show signs of going too far. You may have to deal not only with actual flirtation, but more commonly with children who attempt to subvert your control by over-friendliness; this may especially be a problem in schools or classes where there is an emphasis on cooperative relations between teachers and children (Denscombe 1980a). Flirtation may start with over-friendliness and can become a more extreme problem. You should preferably deal with it in its early stages; the same tactics may be effective at this stage as can be used to deal with the over-friendly child. We will therefore look at flirtation first, as it raises the issues more clearly.

We must stress that the advice in this section relates to secondary pupils. Flirtation is hardly a problem with children below puberty and while older primary children may be intentionally over-friendly, over-friendly or dependent behaviour is more likely to be genuinely motivated with younger children, who will need support rather than repulsion. The teacher of older children will also encounter some with emotional problems who will need to be given greater leeway. You will do well to check with colleagues who know your class if there are any of these you should watch out for.

In many ways flirtation is likely to be more of a problem for male than female teachers, because of the similarity between the conventional male role in courtship and the teacher's role. Male postures and behaviour in flirtation resemble those of dominance (Scheflen and Scheflen 1972). However, women normally take the initiative in starting the interaction by inviting attention; this somewhat resembles the pupil role. Women tend to be very much more aware of the signals they use and their effect, while men often lack conscious awareness of how the relationship is regulated. The situation is complicated because flirtation shades into 'quasi-courtship' (also covered by Scheflen and Scheflen); the same signals are used, but the conversation is kept at the level of mere friendliness by 'cutting off' whenever it seems likely to become too intimate. 'Cut-off' is achieved by looking away or talking to someone else, or by other members of the group breaking into the conversation. Adults are usually skilled at maintaining good relations without excessive intimacy, but adolescents are likely to be less skilled, especially in interpreting the limits of quasi-courtship.

The typical patterns of flirtation pose different problems for male and female teachers. For the female teacher the threat is in some ways more apparent and more clearly demands action. As we have seen in the case of touch, boys seem to react to female teachers in terms of their femaleness. The conventional female role does not involve dominant behaviour in a courtship situation. So long as the female teacher maintains a degree of overt dominance and active control, normal flirtation patterns, which would imply a responsive role, are ruled out. The most appropriate tactics may vary with the age and cooperativeness of the boys.

Younger boys, or older boys from difficult or disruptive classes, may adopt two strategies. They may challenge a female teacher's dominance directly (e.g. Beynon 1985); or by treating her as a woman they destroy her status as a teacher. Beynon describes a range of outright disobedience and insulting behaviour which aims to put the teacher on the defensive by challenging the usefulness of her subject and her ability to teach it; as a woman, she cannot be a 'real' teacher. Boys using this strategy present a serious but clear-cut discipline problem, often when the teacher is working with the whole class rather than individuals. As Beynon indicates, overcoming boys' opposition can be a serious problem; but the firm but friendly teacher who can do this is seen as 'just like a man, not really like a woman teacher at all', according to some of the boys in his study. This may not be quite the compliment she had hoped for, but it is better than some of the alternatives! Alternatively boys may 'over-accept' your friendly approaches, by treating them as invitations to familiarity or flirtation. Here the female teacher is in a similar situation to her male colleagues, and the tactics we discuss below for them apply to her too. The female teacher needs to deal promptly but firmly with any attempt by boys to dominate the classroom, whatever its origins, particularly keeping an eye out for the combination of dominant and playful behaviour. If you deal with the patterns of pupil dominant behaviour described in Chapter 5, you should be able to maintain your authority over the class. Authority, perhaps tempered for younger classes by the playful approach described above in the case of Ms Clemenceau, is the best approach. However, younger female teachers, especially, find quasi-courtship can be useful in establishing effective relationships with cooperative older classes.

The male teacher's necessary behaviour, as a teacher, in dominating and taking the initiative in the classroom, while maintaining friendly relationships with the class, is sufficiently similar to the courtship role for a possibility of confusion to arise. In addition, because the male courtship role does not involve the regulation of relationships to such a large extent, you may find it difficult to become aware of where the problems in signalling arise. You may be anxious to avoid hurting some girls by scornfully rejecting what may be genuine 'crushes', while aware that others may take advantage by embarrassing over-friendliness.

What cues should you, as a male teacher, look out for in detecting and avoiding flirtation? For the male teacher, as we have said, dominance cannot be avoided as part of the teacher role; but you need to politely but firmly decline any inviting behaviour from the girls, just as your female colleagues need to avoid being inviting.

For obvious reasons, there is little information on flirtatious behaviour in the classroom context, either from direct observation or from questionnaire studies. Studies in other contexts indicate that female invitation patterns fall into two groups: an accentuation of friendly behaviour, and sexually inviting behaviour. Girls initially use ambiguous non-verbal signals during flirtation, to avoid over-committing themselves, and these mainly fall into the 'friendly' group. It is obviously desirable if possible for you to deal with the approach at a friendly level: if the girl's behaviour is genuine, she will be less seriously hurt, and if it is not, there is less risk to discipline.

Figure 9.7 The girl has invaded the teacher's personal space, and, as she is standing, she has the advantage of height and freedom of movement (compare Figure 9.3). Her hands-on-hips posture is slightly threatening, and as it pulls her jacket open, 'provocative' in both senses of the word. Her faint smile and approach from behind suggest this is a teasing approach, designed to make the teacher feel uncomfortable, rather than a genuine flirtation

'Friendly' flirtatious behaviour involves slightly more extreme versions of the normal friendly patterns. Initially the girl may simply stand close to the man she hopes to attract or gaze at him. There are obvious difficulties in distinguishing these patterns from work-oriented behaviour; girls may validly behave in this way if they want to raise queries about their work. In courtship the approach is closer and the gaze more sustained, but the differences are relatively subtle (Figure 9.7). Normally listeners look more than speakers, and if you are spending a long time talking about a problem related to the work, this is likely to be reflected in sustained looking by the girl. However, repeated requests for attention, beyond what would normally be required by the work, may arouse suspicions. Excessive animation is a clearer sign; in flirtation girls encourage the relationship by laughing, smiling, gesticulating, nodding and leaning close (Marsh 1988). At this level the behaviour needs care in interpretation as the difference is one of degree (as it has to be in normal flirtation, if the girl is to avoid committing herself too quickly). You need to restrain your natural delight that you are at last getting through – are Latin verbs really that wonderful? Excessive interest which directly relates to what you are saying probably indicates 'genuine' flirtation, as this is the normal pattern outside the classroom – the girl encourages the relationship by approving of the boy. Postural echo (Figure 9.8) frequently occurs in social and flirtatious discussions as an indicator that the partners are 'on the same wavelength' (Bull 1983). In the classroom, where the roles of teacher and student are usually differentiated and the relationship relatively impersonal, it may indicate excessive interest.

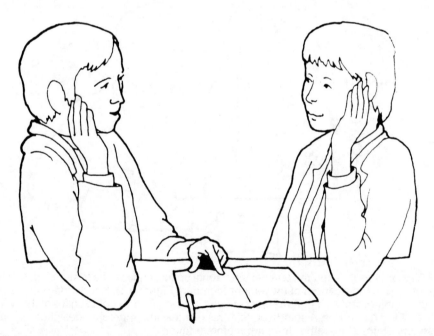

Figure 9.8 Postural echo takes many forms; adults may synchronise their bodily postures, hand positions, or movements such as hair grooming. It demonstrates that a pair (who may be of the same sex) are 'on the same wavelength', and is therefore used by friends. It is therefore available as a sign of affinity during flirtation, and this is probably the most likely use in the classroom context

Explicitly inviting behaviour represents a higher level of commitment; in genuine flirtation it is likely to follow a period of friendly behaviour, or be restricted to the milder forms mentioned below. Girls who are using flirtation to embarrass the teacher are more likely to move directly to clear-cut inviting behaviour with a speed which would normally be inappropriate – it is often at this stage that you become aware that something is wrong. Mild forms of invitation include the coy expression and hand-to-mouth, especially when giggling (Figure 4.1). Both these involve ambivalent behaviour, the girl 'failing' to hide her interest. She thus makes it clear that she is interested, without overtly doing so. A second group of inviting movements emphasise female characteristics such as hair or breasts (Figure 9.7). More explicitly, the girl may touch during flirtation, either by 'failing' to maintain distance so that she apparently accidentally bumps into the teacher or is bumped into, or by actually reaching out (Figure. 9.5, 9.6). In the case illustrated, the teacher cut off the contact by failing to meet the girl's gaze and by actually moving away.

This points out the general principle that disinterest is shown by reversing the signals of interest we have just been discussing – avoiding eye contact, failing to give signals of attention or approval such as nodding or smiling in response to the other person's talk, and by becoming involved with another member of the class. The last is a useful strategy, because children's general expectation that you should be fair to all allows you to point out that other class members need their fair share of attention. By re-emphasising your neutral role as teacher, you can remind the child that their relationship is professional rather than intimate. This strategy applies to the over-friendly child of either sex, who can be reminded both of your role and of their own – to apply themselves to the work, which is the *raison d'être* of school.

The most desirable response to over-friendliness may be to ensure that children recognise your dominance at an early stage. This is not to say that you should be unfriendly – far from it. Beynon (1985) describes an extremely successful teacher who adopted this approach – 'Mr Jovial'. Though he engaged in a considerable amount of joking and teasing, this was not directed at the children personally – for example, when first calling the roll he made jokes about their names but not about their appearance. He did not allow children to make derogatory remarks about each other or to joke about things he had said. We can see a similar process in Mr Weathering's response to an incorrect answer in his first lesson (Chapter 7). In both cases the message which is being transmitted is first, that the classroom will not be too serious a place. Secondly, it will not be threatening, either: the teacher will not challenge children's dignity or allow others to challenge it (provided, of course, they cooperate). Thirdly, this structure is one provided and controlled by the teacher.

SUMMARY

Work with individual children draws more on normal social skills than the more extreme or theatrical signals used for whole-class work. However, as teacher you must take the initiative in approaching and interacting with children more than would be the case in an informal social setting. Attention and interest are shown by getting close to children at their own level; kneeling down also allows you to watch effectively for disruption by other members of the class. Touch is a valuable positive signal, especially with younger children. Older children may resent it, and may in turn use touch or excessive proximity to harass the teacher. This behaviour is best dealt with at an early stage by adopting a more distant relationship.

The training materials explore the meaning of different types of touch, possible risks attached to using them, and the contexts in which they can make a useful contribution to effective classroom interaction. They also deal with the appropriate posture for a teacher who wishes to join an informal group of children.

TRAINING MATERIALS

Many of the anxieties of teaching arise through the desire most of us have to do the best for the children in our charge. This desire will naturally lead to our forming attachments from time to time, either with whole classes, or individual pupils within them. It is even possible, even though we know it is irrational, to form an almost pathological dislike of any individual who disrupts, diverts or in any way damages this special relationship with a class.

In the early days of teaching, a class that actually allows you to teach them with the minimum of diversions is often regarded as 'heaven-sent'; a reward for good deeds in a past life perhaps, or an immeasurable piece of luck, depending on your particular level of paranoia! In any event, your approach to such a favoured class is likely to be far more relaxed, open and friendly.

The use of non-verbal signals by both pupil and teacher can be essential and powerful ingredients in the establishment and maintenance of a friendly working atmosphere, but if wrongly or inappropriately applied they can be equally disturbing and destructive, leading to the development of mutual distrust.

Pictorial Exercise – 'A touch difficult!'

Question 1   The three pictures in Figures 9.9–9.11 show similarly relaxed situations, almost informal in their setting. In each case, however, the teacher has chosen a deliberate positioning ploy.

For each, try to assess the signal being broadcast by the teacher. Do any seem inappropriate to a classroom situation? What would be the likely response from the pupils to each?

Question 2   Figure 9.12 shows a friendly touching exchange of the sort we frequently see between two pupils, but in this case being carried out by a female teacher.

Would you regard this exchange as dangerous in any respect? What would be the likely response of the pupil?

Would the situation be similar if it involved a male teacher? Is there any situation within an educational environment where you would see Figure 9.12 as permissible or acceptable?

Question 3   How do you interpret the group of pupils shown in Figure 9.13?   There is a gap at the front right where a teacher could join the group. Which of the four postures shown in Figure 9.14–9.17 would be most appropriate, and what would the teacher achieve by adopting this posture?

Figure 9.9

Figure 9.10

Figure 9.11

Figure 9.12

Figure 9.13

Figure 9.14

Figure 9.15

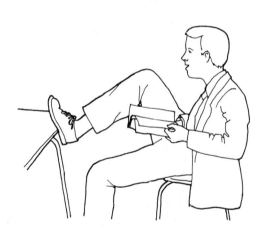

Figure 9.16

Figure 9.17

Descriptive Exercise – 'All for one and one for all'

There will be many occasions in our teaching careers when we feel deeply protective towards certain individual pupils. Numerous situations can give rise to this emotion: bullying, fear, frustration, isolation, all will tug at the heart strings from time to time, but coping with children's special educational needs will almost always lead to the formation of a closer relationship.

This exercise precisely concerns this problem. Anthony is a slow learner. He is fifteen, but has a reading age of just eight. He has come from an emotionally deprived background and is generally suspicious of others, including the majority of his peers. He also demonstrates an extremely low level of dexterity and is often ridiculed by other members of the class during Art and Technology lessons, where he clearly struggles with any practical task.

On this occasion Anthony is involved in a lesson in personal and social education. The theme is 'work and training' and the teacher, Mr Polymath, is trying to involve all the pupils in a discussion about the various types of training on offer.

Mr Polymath is fully sympathetic with Anthony's problems, but, as Anthony has insisted in sitting on his own on this occasion, Mr Polymath is finding it increasingly difficult to involve him. Mr Polymath is soon aware that the class have effectively isolated Anthony, causing him considerable distress. Realising that the only solution is to involve Anthony and readmit him to the fold, Mr Polymath takes a risk and insists on a reply from Anthony during the next round of questions. Mr Polymath makes his move when talking about day release: 'Now we all know about on the job training, but is it still possible to go to college for this training whilst you are at work?'

'Yes sir', replies one boy, 'you can be released for a day to go to college, that's what my sister does.'

'Good', says Mr Polymath, who has moved up to the boy in question and briefly places a hand on his shoulder. 'but what do we call it when we attend college for one day a week?'

'Day release sir', says the boy.

'Right', says Mr Polymath, patting the boy once on the same shoulder, 'excellent, day release – one day a week, see, it makes sense, doesn't it.'

Mr Polymath now moved to Anthony, and walking around behind him he playfully placed his arm around his neck in a mock wrestler's hold.

'What, then, Anthony do we call it when we go to college for a block of time? Remember for a day it's called D–A–Y release, so for a block what will it be called?' The whole class went quiet in irreverent expectation.

'Block', said Anthony looking down at the desk in front of him.

'Good', said Mr Polymath, pretending to increase his hold round Anthony. 'But B–L–O–C–K what?'

'Release', replied Anthony.

'Brilliant', said Mr Polymath, 'spot on', and with that he released his mock hold and briefly squeezed Anthony's shoulders.

'He's right, of course', said Mr Polymath, returning to the rest of the class. 'Let's write that one up on the board.'

During the remainder of the lesson Mr Polymath mentioned 'block release' on several more occasions, each time referring to the fact that Anthony had provided the correct expression.

Question 1   Mr Polymath took several calculated gambles during this exchange in order to involve Anthony. What were the risks involved?

Question 2   Why do you think Mr Polymath used a physical approach in addition to the verbal? How did this physical involvement help in increasing Anthony's status with his peers?

Question 3   Why did Anthony not react negatively or violently to Mr Polymath's neck hold? How did Mr Polymath ensure that it was an acceptable move before making it?

TEACHING MATERIALS – ANSWERS TO EXERCISES

Figure 9.9   Directing touch; returning a boy who has been getting a pen to his seat. Most children saw this teacher as 'friendly', or made other positive comments. Indeed, providing that mutual signals of friendliness are present, this approach should cause few problems. However, if the pupil concerned is in dispute with the teacher and is reluctant to move, then this action could prove dangerous. Pupils, particularly senior pupils, are often full of playground folklore and 'you can't touch me' is something that a difficult pupil may be well aware of. Robertson advises, and we would agree, that in such cases a really close approach, which cannot be challenged in the same way, is better. The pupil is likely to move away in the direction you want, to avoid being crowded.

Figure 9.10   Affection touch and head cant; drawing a child's attention in a practical lesson. Almost all children saw this teacher as 'fun', 'friendly' or 'easy-going'. Most children are instinctively aware of what constitutes 'friendly touch', and this is a particularly good example. The single hand on the near shoulder is not a holding or restraining move (the girl can move away if she wants), and the near shoulder implies closeness. This move is used effectively by female teachers to boys up to the younger secondary age-groups, as the shoulder is a neutral area. However, you may like to consider the implications if this were a male teacher. Touching a child of the opposite sex is always a difficult area and the policy should be, 'if in serious doubt – don't'. This is discussed more fully in the text of the chapter.

Figure 9.11   Affection touch; congratulating for good work. Many children saw this teacher as 'friendly' or 'helpful'. This is quite a comforting move, and particularly effective in encouraging pupils who are struggling with the task. It replaces the hair ruffling that is so often practised with very young children (the acceptability of touch to the head decreases very sharply with age), but as with this activity, it can irritate or cause withdrawal, if for any reason the pupil distrusts the move. Children exposed to physical abuse at home may be suspicious of this gesture and other apparently friendly moves.

Figure 9.12   The point of this particular exercise is probably quite clear to you; touch is a difficult behaviour in the classroom, owing to the problems of interpretation. Where touch occurs in direct relation to the task (in PE, for example), it is accepted. Where its purpose is not clear it is a dangerous activity. The problem is further exacerbated by the different interpretations of the same actions by male as opposed to female teachers. Overt displays of affection by female teachers are often seen as more acceptable (reflecting the situation in society in general) and in this context 'touch' can generate a feeling of security and warmth within the pupil. The male teacher, on the other hand, is more likely to be burdened with suspect intent. Boys, particularly older boys, may see 'touch' by a male teacher as being aggressive or threatening. A far more serious charge may be made by both male and female pupils if they interpret touch as sexual.

   This danger is clearly illustrated by Figure 9.12. Placing a hand on a shoulder of another, particularly the near shoulder; is usually regarded as acceptable (Figure 9.10). When activity-directed, it may help to reinforce or to comfort when difficulty is being experienced. In this case, however, there is no obvious reason to touch. Gaze and postural orientation give no clues as to why this is an appropriate gesture, as the boy is not attending to his work and there is no shared focus of attention. The situation is wide open to interpretation, particularly misinterpretation: a passing touch like this between pupils would be seen as flirtatious. Compare Figure 4.5, where the more dominant behaviour of the teacher and the shared focus meant that the move was accepted in the way it was intended.

Figure 9.13   This shows a group of pupils in relaxed conversation. Their gaze and postural orientation indicate their involvement with the conversation, with no apparent dominant gestures indicating challenge within the group.

Figure 9.14   Here the teacher is using postural echo to gain acceptance within this group. The desk sit with the forward lean and open posture signal involvement, and most children saw this teacher positively, for instance as 'helpful' and 'fun'. In this respect he should fit into the pattern of the group, being accepted without losing his given authority. However, this posture is a characteristically male one, and less suitable for a woman, unless she is wearing a long skirt; Figure 9.17 would be a better alternative.

Figure 9.15   Desk sit, in a closed, tense posture, with some tendency to shuffle around on his seat. Such a posture might be adopted by someone under stress, for example an interview candidate. He looks less than comfortable in this group setting and this will place him outside the group. The compound effect may be to erode any authority he might have held, as he falls between two stools; on the one hand he is trying to enter a more or less egalitarian group – a move which itself brings him down towards the level of the pupils – but is unlikely to be accepted, while on the other, his weak, nervous stance may erode any authority he already possessed. He would have done better to have stood back from the group, allowing a more formal distance to reinforce his position.

Figure 9.16   This posture could have two consequences, neither being particularly helpful. If the group were anti-authoritarian they might see his behaviour as adding strength to their position, thereby eroding his authority with the group. It shows, through the foot on the table and casual lean, scant respect for the traditional postures of authority adopted by most teachers. Alternatively, he may be rejected by the group for using signals that they feel are rightly theirs within the classroom situation. If this group see themselves as somewhat distant from the role of the teacher (as do most pupils) they will find the 'closeness' advertised in this approach as being false, out of place or even embarrassing. In either case the teacher here is likely to lose a number of brownie points!

Figure 9.17   Leaning back against a cupboard is a relaxed posture which preserves dominance through height. The positions of arms and legs give stability, but also slightly increase the size of the body, again contributing unobtrusively to dominance. This is the standing posture equivalent to 9.14 and gives the same impression of calm amiable control, without any problems of decency. (In fact this figure is based on a videotape of a male teacher.)

Descriptive Exercise – 'All for one and one for all'

Question 1

Mr Polymath took a number of risks in his approach to this lesson but the chances were, as an experienced teacher, that he knew what they were. His first problem concerned Anthony's isolation from the group, and the need to involve him more whilst ensuring no further loss of confidence. The first gamble concerned the amount of physical contact involved, in holding Anthony around the neck and appearing to throttle him should he get the question wrong. Anthony must have sensed the playful intent behind this move and decided to go along. Had he reacted adversely there could have been a particularly difficult, if not violent, situation. This approach would not work for an inexperienced teacher or one who had not yet established relationships.

The second risk centred around Anthony's answer; after all he could have got it wrong! Mr Polymath knew this, but obviously wished to use the same ploy – literally a physical link – as he had with the remainder of the class; but if Anthony had got the answer wrong his isolation would have been greater and tinged with ridicule after such a build-up. Mr Polymath relied on his own natural understanding, his firm, yet relaxed approach to the class and his obvious charisma to ensure that the risk paid off.

Question 2

Physical involvement, particularly rough and tumble, can be useful, especially with a group of boys, although it is more usual on a playing field or in a youth club. Under-achieving pupils may be very physical in their nature, living more by their emotions than their academic prowess. By deliberately using touch, patting the boys, holding their shoulders etc., Mr Polymath was attempting to break down barriers between himself and the boys. Touch used in this way, carefully and with full consideration of the possible consequences, can help to pull a group together and generate empathy and confidence between all concerned. This is particularly true if touch is used in relation to a task and as a reward for having achieved a correct answer. It was important that Mr Polymath used the same approach with Anthony as with other members of the class if he was to draw him back into the fold. Getting a question right held high status in Mr Polymath's lessons, but receiving an additional pat on the shoulder or arm was an even greater sign of success. Anthony may not have received many of these rewarding gestures in the past; all the more important that he should on this occasion. Having done so, his status with his peers increased considerably as he had become one of the publicly successful.

Question 3

Mr Polymath's approach was successful largely because he had established a reputation as a charismatic teacher through moves such as complete fairness in dealing with pupils. The class clearly understood that there was no ulterior motive behind his approach and that his sole concern was to help them improve their understanding of his subject; no threat, no negative intent, and certainly no sexual overtones. Anthony did not react to Mr Polymath's armhold because it was consistent with the approach that he had used with others – and indeed an example of the fairness mentioned above. By placing his arm around Anthony's neck Mr Polymath had 'upped the stakes', gambling that Anthony would come up with the goods in terms of the correct answer. As he moved towards the point of the whole exercise, so he increased the extent of physical contact, having ensured that it was an acceptable move by using it consistently with all members of the class.

This type of approach can be extremely dangerous and it is not recommended for any teacher who has not had a long and successful history of control and empathy with the class. When used by established teachers and in this positive way, touch is one of the most powerful non-verbal tools at our disposal. Perhaps it is a comment on society that we are unable to use it as readily as we could. This indicates the distance that often exists between us as teachers and the pupils that we so desperately want to support.

Chapter 10

Implications for trainers

In this chapter we look at three issues: how non-verbal skills are best trained, how they normally develop in new teachers, and evidence of their importance. We then discuss how trainers can apply non-verbal skills in practice, and give examples of half- and whole-day programmes suitable for school-based INSET.

HOW NON-VERBAL SKILLS ARE BEST TRAINED

In this book we have emphasised specific skills and contexts in which they may be used, and given suggestions for sessions based on these. This approach is based on Klinzing and associates' work in Germany, and their survey of the research literature (e.g. Klinzing and Tisher 1986) – unfortunately this reference is not very readily available, though it is discussed in Neill (1991a).

Klinzing distinguishes between two basic types of training. The first attempts to train general skills or dispositions such as enthusiasm or empathy. The research suggests that this type is generally ineffective. The second type, training in specific skills, is therefore adopted in this book. Provided this is done satisfactorily, training in specific skills not only increases the use of the specific skills, but can also increase related specific or general skills. For example, training in the specific skills of voice delivery, eye contact and gestures led to a general increase in warmth, interest, activity and assurance. Increases in skill could lead to measurable improvements in children's performance, such as an increase in correct answers or other measures of achievement. As most of the studies were experimental, there is limited evidence on how long the effects last. In most cases follow-up periods were short, though a few studies indicated the persistence of training effects for up to three months.

Satisfactory outcomes require a reasonable duration for the courses; Klinzing found that if courses were too short they had little effect. Successful courses included all or most of four elements:

1 an explanatory structure, usually theoretically based;
2 illustration or demonstration of the particular skills being trained, often via film or video;
3 opportunity for participants to practice;
4 feedback on performance.

We have aimed to provide elements 1 and 2 in this book, with activities suggested for 3 and 4.

HOW NON-VERBAL TEACHING SKILLS ARE ACQUIRED

We would expect teachers who have passed through a four-year training course to have developed many of the non-verbal skills specific to teachers during their periods of teaching practice: teachers who have been through a PGCE, or licensed or articled teachers, are likely to continue to learn on the job for some time. However, this assumes that teacher training courses contain adequate sections on teaching skills. Some of our own earlier research indicated that, at least in our sample, neither third-year student teachers nor probationer teachers (with a few exceptions) had useful input on non-verbal classroom management skills on their courses. This may have changed with the recent greater emphasis on classroom skills in teacher training, but there is limited evidence for this.

The evidence suggests that those who already have developed appropriate non-verbal interpersonal skills before entering teacher training are better able to benefit from their teaching experiences. This may be because they are more perceptive and pick out relevant parts of their experiences and learn from them. Alternatively, more perceptive student teachers may have more positive, enlightening and rewarding experiences, while their unfortunate contemporaries are sucked uncomprehending into the maelstrom without ever being quite able to work out what hit them.

There is some evidence that more expressive and non-verbally confident PGCE applicants do better on the course and are better able to get jobs. They are also more likely to be successful applicants in the first place. More effective student teachers were more perceptive of children's non-verbal signals of understanding (shown on video), and more aware of their own signals (Lawes 1987a, 1987b). Lawes found that this was specific to their age-specialisation, which suggests that these were skills learnt during training.

Awareness was more clearly related to success for secondary student teachers, who are involved in more work with whole-class groups of more recalcitrant pupils than primary teachers, and therefore have to draw more on their theatrical and present-ational skills. However, the secondary students were less able to interpret the videotapes, which showed junior children, than their primary colleagues. As children's use of non-verbal signals changes with age, experience of the specific age-group seemed to be necessary for optimum decoding. Secondary children tend to be more devious and subtle in their use of non-verbal signals and the secondary teachers may therefore have over-interpreted the signals of primary children.

Some of this skill may be under conscious control; thus Calderhead (1986) found that among primary student teachers, those who saw their lessons as a 'performance', separate from their true selves, did better than those who were more personally involved. This implies both greater self-confidence and a greater awareness of what they were doing.

A critical point is that conscious awareness does not necessarily increase with experience after a certain point; indeed, the opposite may happen, as classroom skills become routinised and automatic. The level of effort put into teaching practice could not be sustained over a whole career. This fits the general pattern that as a skill – for instance driving – becomes 'over-learned', it is moved down to unconscious, automatic channels. Awareness may increase with experience early on, but decrease later. Thus there was no relation between non-verbal awareness and assessed teaching skill among third-year student teachers, but more effective probationer teachers showed more awareness of non-verbal signals. However, experienced teachers were actually less non-verbally perceptive than newly qualified ones under test conditions. They may well compensate for this by more detailed knowledge of the pupils and situations they are normally dealing with, so they do not normally need to look at each incident with the same attention as their less experienced colleagues.

This lies behind Smith and Tomlinson's (1984) suggestion that experienced teachers may not be the best people to train new teachers, as they have lost conscious access to their own skills. The experienced teachers may also feel that these skills are trivial in comparison to the aspects of classroom life which now occupy their conscious thoughts. However, we feel that expert teaching is impossible without a foundation of these skills, and we hope that this book will have been useful in laying that foundation.

THE RELATIVE IMPORTANCE OF NON-VERBAL COMMUNICATION

How important *is* non-verbal communication to teachers? A moment's consideration shows that the curriculum content of a lesson, which is after all its *raison d'être*, is transmitted almost entirely verbally. It would be easy to tell what a lesson is about from a pure audio recording, very difficult from a pure video recording, unless the teacher was an expansive gesturer talking about a visually oriented subject. Only the writing on the blackboard, hardly 'non-verbal' as we have considered it here, would be more accessible from the video recording. However, the example of Ms Discord, quoted in the introduction, and many others in our experience, shows that well-prepared, and even well-verbalised content, does not guarantee success; non-verbal pzazz gets the message across – but how much?

The answer is complicated because non-verbal communication is only a part of what goes on in the classroom, and because of its spontaneous nature. The same message can usually be conveyed by several alternative combinations of non-verbal signals, and very often it seems to be the context in which the signal is given that is critical, rather than the particular signal used. Further, signals may be redundant, so that while a signal would be responded to in isolation, it would be ignored if it was, as normal, combined with another signal. In the classroom, we cannot therefore expect a clear one-to-one link between outcomes and particular signals. Thus we saw in Chapter 2 that a mild signal given from close to has the same effect as an intense one given from further away.

In practice, as implied by Gannaway (1976), it is likely that acceptance by the class involves the teacher going through a series of hurdles, at each of which different types of signal are of importance. As Gannaway indicates, and as we have suggested in this book, the first hurdle is whether the teacher can keep order, the second whether she can make the material interesting. If she also shows affability and a sense of humour, according to Gannaway, she 'has it made', and other aspects of her behaviour can vary widely without interfering with her relationship with the children.

The fact that non-verbal signals are normally spontaneous creates problems in designing experiments to assess how much they contribute, as is clear from Woolfolk's work (reported in Bull 1983). To assess the relative importance of verbal and non-verbal communication, she had a pair of student teachers presenting the same lesson to different classes, varying the verbal and non-verbal feedback between classes. The problem with this approach (apart from the question of whether student teachers were as effective teachers and signallers as experienced teachers) is that the lessons read as somewhat artificial even in the report, and no doubt seemed even more artificial to the twelve-year-old children to whom they were presented. If the influence of non-verbal communication relies on being perceived as a more reliable indicator of the sender's unconscious feelings than verbal communication, it is likely that children of this age would have been aware of the artificiality of the whole situation, and would have adjusted their responses accordingly. It is difficult to see what Woolfolk could have done to overcome this criticism. An alternative approach would have been to observe a range of teachers teaching the same curriculum content. This regularly occurs in schools and was included in our video study. The differing success of colleagues working with the same material clearly indicates the importance of the presentational factors we have been discussing in this book. Unfortunately colleagues differ in a range of ways, and it then becomes difficult to tell just what are the decisive factors.

Woolfolk found that the quality of children's work was influenced more by the verbal content than by the accompanying non-verbal signals. The children tended to do better when the teacher's non-verbal cues were negative (frowning, head-shaking and voice tone) and the most effective combination was 'firm' (positive comments delivered with negative non-verbal cues). The least effective combination was 'apologetic' (negative comments delivered with positive non-verbal cues).

The relative importance of non-verbal signals may also depend on the interest of the material and children's enthusiasm for it, Klinzing suggests. Thus non-verbal signals seem to be relatively less important in the primary school, where children are more cooperative. They tend also at this age to attend relatively more to verbal signals, in any case. Children may also take more notice of non-verbal signals for some types of message (e.g. how positive the teacher feels about them) and attend more to verbal signals for others (e.g. the grades the teacher is likely to give) – so far as we can judge from questionnaire work on American high school children (reported in Bull 1983).

PRACTICAL APPLICATION

Non-verbal communication and the INSET programme

When writing this book we were acutely aware of the overlap between non-verbal communication and other areas of the teaching spectrum. Teaching and learning styles, disaffection, special needs, all have aspects which relate to non-verbal behaviours, in addition to the more specific area of class control on which this book concentrates. It is precisely because of this multi-dimensional quality that we feel that non-verbal communication should have a place on the INSET agenda.

There will be pitfalls, of course, for any institution hoping to make this move. Firstly there will almost certainly be those on the staff who feel uneasy about the topic. Their concern will be legitimate and will range from a suspicion that this is all part of the latest 'buzz' craze, to a deep and genuine fear of exploring this aspect of their classroom style. Such fears must be taken seriously and catered for, if the topic is to be presented effectively and made worthwhile.

Then there will be those who feel that they can use the time more effectively in preparation for the National Curriculum, Key Stage planning, or simply dealing with departmental issues. Their claim is also legitimate and they may need some convincing if they are to avoid the feeling of having been press-ganged into the programme.

So let us look at these extreme reactions and work towards the middle ground. As far as we are aware there has been little attempt in educational circles to tackle the topic, even though 'Body Language' has been avidly promoted from time to time in the media, perhaps to the point of overkill. Unlike the tabloid tips, however, we do not pretend that, by using a few simple techniques, you and your colleagues will be transformed into enigmatic, charismatic 'leaders of men', able to exert phenomenal power over all pupils – unfortunately! We are suggesting that by increasing your *awareness* of non-verbal behaviours you may improve your teaching, enhance your performance and reduce some of the stress that accumulates when relying on verbal patterns alone. It is a tall order, but it begins with a willingness to listen and consider the possibilities.

A more serious hurdle may be faced in trying to allay the fears of those staff who will feel threatened by having to face consciously what they may be doing subconsciously. Feeling a fool is one thing, but looking one is quite another matter. Again, when suggesting the topic for INSET it is worth acknowledging this fact and assuring the staff that there will be no question of 'spying' or, worse, of playing candid camera. The exercises have been so designed as to call on the collective knowledge of the audience, by involving them in familiar situations. There is no suggestion of right and wrong; more often it is a case of cause and effect. The audience can involve themselves in the exercises, develop them through discussion, use anecdotes and suggest solutions, all without exposing themselves to the critical eye of the videocamera, unless they wish to do so at a later stage.

What of those in the middle ground? Is this likely to be more beneficial than National Curriculum planning? It would be too glib to trot out the answer, 'You get out what you put in!', though it no doubt applies. It is true to say, however, that those teachers constantly in the thick of it, involved in planning, preparation, analysis, statistics, SATS etc. need, more than ever before, the complete repertoire of classroom skills at their disposal. Containing classes engaged in active work whilst compiling assessments can only be achieved by understanding the complete dynamics of classroom behaviour. It may not save you time, but it might help reduce the stress.

Our case then is fairly clear; we believe that non-verbal communication has a valid and useful role within a whole school INSET programme. Our experience, from running training sessions on non-verbal communication in schools and for probationer and student teachers, shows that staff will respond and even enjoy looking at the associated phenomena, once they feel that it has a place in their professional lives.

Structuring the programme

Time is always at a premium on INSET days, and having decided to include non-verbal communication on the agenda it then falls to someone to structure the programme and make the most effective use of the time available.

The programme you construct may reflect, to some extent, the other issues present in the school development plan. If, for example, there is a need to look at special needs teaching then there are certain chapters in this book which would be immediately relevant. Similarly, if the school were looking at teaching and learning styles and the development of active learning, then again some areas of the book may be more suitable than others. If you take this approach it would be fair to say that for many schools, particularly those which are just developing INSET policy, a half-day session may be a safer bet. If, on the other hand, you are planning to run two teacher days consecutively, spending a whole day on 'communication skills' may serve as a useful introduction to a variety of topics on the following day.

To help with the problem of planning, we have suggested below two possible programmes, one half-day, one whole-day. In addition we have included a set of leader notes for the member of staff who draws the short straw and has to present the session. These programmes have worked under school conditions without support or input brought in from outside, and whilst we accept that there can be no guarantee that their success will be duplicated, we feel confident that the majority of teachers will find their contents worthwhile, if not entertaining. They use the training materials at the end of the earlier chapters, which have been laid out with this purpose in mind. The answers to these materials, which follow each chapter, can be used if required. More detailed guidance about each activity follows the two programmes.

HALF-DAY SESSION

(approximately 9.00 a.m. to 12.30 p.m.)

'Non-verbal Communication in Teaching and Learning'

This half-day session should serve to introduce, or raise awareness of the role of non-verbal communication in the classroom. It is not designed to teach new tricks, provide Granny with a new clutch of eggs, or to fly in the face of accepted 'good practice'. Hopefully it will be seen as an additional tool at colleagues' disposal that may be applied to a variety of situations.

9.00 a.m. Introductory overview:

Why are we here?
What do we hope to learn?

9.15 a.m. Introduction:

a. How do we display disinterest and enthusiasm in everyday life?
b. How do we show anger and compassion in our relationships?
c. How do we display authority and status towards our colleagues?

9.45 a.m. What do we know at the outset?:

Report back from first session

10.00 a.m. Can we apply this to the classroom?:

Issue of materials for workshops

10.15 a.m. Workshops on the following:

a. 'Check in on arrival' – setting the scene (Chapter 3)
b. 'Are you receiving me?' – getting attention (Chapter 6)
c. 'Entertaining the troops' – displaying enthusiasm (Chapter 7)
d. 'A breakdown in communication?' – dealing with confrontation (Chapter 8)

10.30a.m. Break

11.00 a.m. Continue in workshops

11.30 a.m. Feedback from workshops:

a. What were the answers?
b. Were the concepts/situations recognisable?
c. Developments on the theme

12.00 noon Plenary session:

a. Strategies for increasing self-awareness – can we improve our use of NVC?
b. Pupil behaviours – have they a strategy?
c. Do we need to know more? – use of further INSET time

12.30 p.m. END

WHOLE DAY SESSION

(approximately 9.00 a.m. to 3.30 p.m.)

'Non-verbal Communication – its Power and Place in the Classroom'

9.00 a.m. Introductory overview:

Why are we here?
What do we hope to learn?

9.15 a.m. Introduction:

a. How do we display interest and enthusiasm in everyday life?
b. How do we show anger and compassion in our relationships?
c. How do we display authority and status towards our colleagues?

9.45 a.m. What do we know at the outset?:

Report back from first session

10.00 a.m. Developing our awareness:

a. Signals and Receivers – whole group workshop based upon Chapter 2
b. The nature of challenge – group workshops centring on 'open and closed' challenges outlined in Chapter 4

10.30 a.m. Feedback:

Groups from (b) above report their findings and share thoughts

11.00 a.m. Break

11.30 a.m. Video observations:

(if appropriate to (a); if not, to (b))
a. Observation and comment on two five-minute clips showing contrasting behaviours
b. Selection of overhead transparencies taken from Chapters 3 and 4

11.45 a.m. Feedback and discussion from observations

12.00 noon 'Reading between the lines'

Issue of workshop materials for recognising and using strengths and skills

12.30 p.m. Lunch

1.30 p.m. Workshops on the following:

a. 'Check in on arrival' – setting the scene (Chapter 3)
b. 'Are you receiving me' – getting attention (Chapter 6)
c. 'Entertaining the troops' – displaying enthusiasm (Chapter 7)
d. 'A breakdown in communications?' – dealing with confrontation (Chapter 8)

2.15 p.m. Feedback from workshops

a. What were the answers?
b. Were the concepts/situations recognisable?
c. Developments on the theme

2.45 p.m. Coffee

2.50 p.m. 'From theory into practice':

Fifteen-minute video screening of an actual lesson
a. How much NVC was evident?
b. How much of the day's programme could be recognised?
c. Is NVC more visible now we know where to look?

3.15 p.m. Plenary session:

Feedback on the day

3.30 p.m. END

Leader notes

It is always going to be difficult leading an INSET day on an area for which you may not feel wholly prepared. In a sense that is the purpose of the book, giving teachers, senior or otherwise, a simple and comprehensive grounding in the dynamics of this area.

The programme outlined above has been built around exercises that exist in this book, exercises that can be lifted from the pages and used exactly as they stand. We have also provided a set of 'answers', although in practice we have found that teachers need little help in this respect. On the contrary, they frequently provide a wider understanding and a wealth of anecdotes which will go far beyond what we can offer in the space available.

General situation

It is important for all participants to feel secure throughout. Absolute notions of right and wrong should be avoided and humour should be allowed to permeate wherever possible, as a relaxed staff will be more inclined to give to the programme and discuss their own behaviour patterns.

It often helps if participants receive copies of all the exercises used and not just those on which they are being asked to work. This encourages staff to see overlap where it exists and, more particularly, to contribute to the responses made by others.

The exercise topics suggested are suitable for small or large staff groups. With large numbers it should be possible to give each exercise to two groups, thus benefiting from dual feedback and cross discussion.

The principal difference between the whole and half-day sessions lies in the depth of the treatment of 'open' and 'closed' challenges and the nature of deviancy. This latter concept is crucial to a thorough understanding of the nature of challenge and therefore forms an important section of the whole-day programme. However, for the shorter session it is often more valuable to involve the audience with the whole concept of non-verbal behaviour, rather than a hybrid section, particularly as this may lead to a request for more, thereby providing the ideal opportunity to introduce the phenomenon of challenge.

The additional time available with the whole-day programme will also enable the use of video recordings, if this is felt appropriate. There are some difficult issues here, however, and these will be covered later in this section.

Time

The time format suggested should be taken as a guide only, the important feature being the length of time allocated to each activity. A good break is essential and experience shows that it will be used effectively.

Aims of the activities used

These notes indicate the aims behind each of the exercises we have chosen.

'What do you know already?'

Here we are attempting to remind staff of the wealth of knowledge that they already possess, use and understand in their everyday communications.

The suggestions contained in a, b and c are intended to give teachers the opportunity to revisit their existing fund of knowledge by taking part in a role-play exercise and observing their colleagues. Leaders may suggest the following:

For (a) How do we display interest and enthusiasm in everyday life?

Try: Describe a particularly enjoyable play or television programme. Describe your last holiday or a particularly enjoyable moment in your life.

For (b) How do we show anger and compassion in our relationships?

Try: For those that are willing, this is an ideal opportunity to role play an argument, or, perhaps, to play counsellor in a tricky negotiation with a reluctant pupil.

For (c) How do we display authority and status towards our colleagues?

Try: Firstly, role-playing an authority figure outside the teaching profession; a member of the police force, or a senior military officer, both engaged in interviewing someone less sure of their ground. To make things really buzz try being the Head and telling the caretaker that s/he must lose several staff owing to cutbacks.

In order to operate this section, staff should be divided into small groups of three or four, with an observer appointed for each group. The job of the observer should be quite specific: they should record and report evidence of how visual gesture, posture and signal were used to emphasise the nature of the emotion and content of the discussions. It is always possible to have two observers. Groups may rotate within the exercise and the overall observations reported back to the staff as a whole, either on a special pro forma or through the 'brainstorming' technique. Care should be taken to avoid making staff take part if they are concerned in any way, or are particularly self-conscious.

Workshops:

Workshops differ from 'activities' in that they involve staff in the consideration of specific materials or issues on which they should report back. The nature of these exercises is more to do with discussion than with providing 'correct' answers.

The workshop exercises are based entirely on training materials from the book. These materials appear at the end of each chapter and can be photocopied as appropriate. The materials themselves should be entirely self-explanatory, giving the opportunity for discussion both on the micro level in the visual exercises, and on the macro level across the wider field of the descriptive ones. The corresponding answers can be found at the end of each chapter.

Feedback

Feedback is an essential element in the programme, be it whole or half-day. Shared thought and experience serves to add direction and strength to the programme, as well as providing evidence of its validity. Most importantly, feedback provides reassurance. It allows staff to realise that they have a right to their views and that their ideas are both valid and sound. We have found that a great deal of relief can be gained from the realisation that 'I do that' or 'that happens in my lesson'.

Video techniques

The whole-day programme gives the opportunity to use video recording as an additional element. We feel that it can be particularly useful to see the signals of pupil and teacher 'in action', so to speak, and to place them in the overall context of the lesson situation. There are, of course, enormous dangers with using the video, both in terms of its potential effect on the lesson being recorded and the more obvious implications for the member of staff concerned. On the whole, unless the school is particularly avant-garde in this respect, we would suggest the following ground-rules when recording and using video material for INSET:

1 Video material should never be taken or shown without the express permission of the member of staff concerned.
2 Sections or clips to be used should be agreed with the member of staff beforehand.
3 When used for INSET purposes the member of staff involved should have the opportunity to introduce the clip and comment at the end.
4 The recording should be destroyed at the end of the INSET programme unless the member of staff has given written permission for it to be used again.
5 Clips used should come from a wide range of staff, years and subject areas and include senior staff.
6 Comments on the clips should be specific to the nature of the exercise and objectively based.
7 Less disturbance is caused if the camera is mounted on a tripod and used in a fixed position. (This also allows use of a mains adaptor which is more reliable than batteries.) The operator should not talk to the pupils and if possible should be a

technician or other non-teacher. If most of the action is to be in a restricted area, an unattended camera will give good results and can be switched on by the teacher herself.

The success of the INSET programme

It is one thing to plan an INSET programme; quite another to deliver it and respond to the thoughts, feelings and anxieties of those taking part. The programmes we have suggested and the corresponding notes are not set in tablets of stone, and it may well be that those involved in planning INSET, having read the book, will decide to approach the topic from a different angle. However it is approached, we feel that the message is clear: non-verbal communication is a feature of classroom behaviour that cannot be overlooked or ignored. It is part of the fabric of communication that all adults and children use in all situations. Understanding more about how it works will help. It may not cure all problems, develop burning enthusiasm within the class or stop us from losing our tempers from time to time, but in all these respects it will contribute to the solution.

SUMMARY

Training courses should be of adequate length and should contain most of the following four elements: theoretical structure, illustration or demonstration of skills, practice, and feedback. Student teachers who are already socially skilled seem better able to learn new non-verbal skills, probably because of their greater awareness. Awareness is also related to teaching success, though this may be restricted to the age-group of which the teacher has experience, as ages differ in the way they use non-verbal signals. Experienced teachers may have difficulties in communicating which non-verbal skills they use to trainees, because their skills have become automatic and are not usually consciously monitored. Similar problems make it difficult to assess the relative importance of verbal and non-verbal communication under classroom conditions because attempts to control non-verbal communication to allow experimental comparisons are likely to alter the communication and its effects. However, there is some evidence that non-verbal signals are particularly valuable when the subject material is not inherently interesting to the class.

The second section of the chapter is practical guidance for trainers, including dealing with the anxieties and counter-arguments likely to be raised by colleagues. We provide suggestions, based on our own experience, for half-day and full-day training programmes, the latter progressing to more sophisticated skills such as distinguishing between open and closed challenges. We also discuss the problems and issues which may arise in running such programmes.

References

Adams, R. S. and Biddle, B. J. (1970) *Realities of Teaching: Explorations with Videotape*, New York: Holt, Rinehart & Winston.

Atkinson, M. (1984) *Our Masters' Voices*, London: Methuen.

Baldwin, D. and Lister, C. (1987) *Safety When Alone*, Hove: Wayland.

Ball, S. J. (1980) 'Initial encounters in the classroom and the process of establishment', in P. Woods (ed.) *Pupil Strategies*, London: Croom Helm.

Beattie, G. (1983) *Talk: An Analysis of Speech and Non-verbal Behaviour in Conversation*, Milton Keynes: Open University Press.

Bennett, N., Desforges, C., Cockburn, A. and Wilkinson, B. (1984) *The Quality of Pupil Learning Experiences*, London: Lawrence Erlbaum.

Beynon, J. (1985) *Initial Encounters in the Secondary School*, London: Falmer.

Bossert, S. T. (1979) *Tasks and Social Relationships in Classrooms*, Cambridge: Cambridge University Press.

Brazil, D., Coulthard, M. and Johns, C. (1980) *Discourse Intonation and Language Teaching*, London: Longman.

Brown, G. A. and Armstrong, S. (1984) 'Explaining and explanations', in E. C. Wragg (ed.) *Classroom Teaching Skills*, London: Croom Helm.

Brown, G. A. and Edmondson, R. (1984) 'Asking questions', in E. C. Wragg (ed.) *Classroom Teaching Skills*, London: Croom Helm.

Bull, P. (1983) *Body Movement and Interpersonal Communication*, Wiley: Chichester.

Calderhead, J. (1986) 'The contribution of field experience to student primary teachers' professional learning,' paper presented at the Annual Conference of the British Educational Research Association, Bristol, September 1986.

Caswell, C. (1982) 'Pupil strategies affecting classrom control', unpublished M.Ed. thesis, University of Warwick.

Delamont, S. (1976) *Interaction in the Classroom*, London: Methuen.

Denscombe, M. (1980a) ' "Keeping 'em quiet": the significance of noise for the practical activity of teaching,' in P. Woods (ed.) *Teacher Strategies*, London: Croom Helm.

Denscombe, M. (1980b) 'Pupil strategies and the open classroom', in P. Woods (ed.) *Pupil Strategies* London: Croom Helm.

Docking, J. W. (1980) *Control and Discipline in Schools*, London: Harper & Row.

Ellis, A. and Beattie, G. (1986) *The Psychology of Language and Communication*, London: Weidenfeld & Nicholson.

Evans, K. (1979) 'A touch of control in the classroom', *New Society* 47: 187–9.

Furlong, V. J. (1976) 'Interaction sets in the classroom; towards a study of pupil knowledge', in M. Stubbs and S. Delamont (eds) *Explorations in Classroom Observation*, London: Wiley.

Galton, M. and Willcocks, J. (1983) *Moving from the Primary Classroom*, London: Routledge & Kegan Paul.

Gannaway, H. (1976) Making sense of school, in M. Stubbs and S. Delamont (eds) *Explorations in Classroom Observation*, London: Wiley.

Goffman, E. (1972) *Relations in Public*, Harmondsworth: Penguin.

Goffman, E. (1979) *Gender Advertisements*, London: Macmillan.

Guy, J. J. (1980) 'An Observational Study of Practical Chemistry Teaching at the First Year University and Sixth-form Levels', unpublished M.Ed.thesis, University of Warwick.

Hall, E. T. (1966) *The Hidden Dimension*, New York: Doubleday.

Humphries, S. (1981) *Hooligans or Rebels?*, Oxford: Basil Blackwell.

Klinzing, H. G. and Tisher, R. I. (1986) 'Expressive nonverbal behaviours; a review of research on training with consequent recommendations for teacher education', in J. D. Raths and L. G. Katz (eds) *Advances in Teacher Education* (Vol. 2.), Norwood, N.J.: Ablex.

Kounin, J. S. (1970) *Discipline and Group Management in Classrooms*, Huntington, N.Y.: Robert E. Krieger.

Lawes, J. S. (1987a) 'The relationship between non-verbal awareness of self and teaching competence in student teachers', *Journal of Education for Teaching* 13: 145–54.

Lawes, J. S. (1987b) 'Student teachers' awareness of pupils' non-verbal responses', *Journal of Education for Teaching* 13: 257–66.

McNeill, D. (1985) So you think gestures are non-verbal? *Psychological Review* 92: 350–71.

McNeill, D. (1986) 'Iconic gestures of children and adults', *Semiotica* 62: 107–28.

Macpherson, J. (1983) *The Feral Classroom*, London: Routledge & Kegan Paul.

Marland, M. (1975) *The Craft of the Classroom*, London: Heinemann.

Marsh, P. (ed.) (1988) *Eye to Eye*, London: Guild.

Marsh, P., Rosser, E. and Harre, R. (1978) *The Rules of Disorder*, London: Routledge & Kegan Paul.

Moore, D. W. and Glynn, T. (1984) 'Variation in question rate as a function of position in the classroom', *Educational Psychology* 4: 233–48.

Morris, D. (1977) *Man-watching*, London: Triad Panther.

Moskowitz, G. and Hayman, J. L. (1974) 'Interaction patterns of first-year, typical and "best" teachers in inner-city schools', *Journal of Educational Research* 67: 224–30.

Moskowitz, G. and Hayman, J. L. (1976) 'Success strategies of inner-city teachers: a year-long study', *Journal of Educational Research* 69: 283–9.

Nash, R. (1974) 'Pupils' expectations for their teachers', *Research in Education* 12: 47–61.

Neill, S. R. St J. (1991a) *Classroom Nonverbal Communication*, London: Routledge.

Neill, S. R. St J. (1991b) 'Children's response to touch – a questionnaire study', *British Educational Research Journal* 17: 149–63.

Neil, S. R. St J., Fitzgerald, J. M. and Jones, B. (1983) 'The relation between reported awareness of non-verbal communication and rated effectiveness in probationer and student teachers', *Journal of Education for Teaching* 9: 16–29.

Partington, J. (1984) *Law and the New Teacher*, London: Holt, Rinehart & Winston.

Pollard, A. (1985) *The Social World of the Primary School*, London: Holt, Rinehart & Winston.

Robertson, J. (1989) *Effective Classroom Control*, London: Hodder & Stoughton.

Rogers, B. (1991) *You Know the Fair Rule*, Harlow: Longman.

Rowe, M. B. (1974) 'Wait time and reward as instructional variables; their influence on language, logic and fate control', *Journal of Research on Science Teaching* 11: 81–94.

Scheflen, A. E. and Scheflen, A. (1972) *Body Language and Social Order*, Englewood Cliffs, N.J.: Prentice-Hall.

Schwebel, A. I. and Cherlin, D. L. (1972) 'Physical and social distancing in teacher–pupil relationships', *Journal of Educational Psychology* 63: 543–50.

Sinclair, J. McN. and Brazil, D. (1982) *Teacher Talk*, Oxford: Oxford University Press.

Sinclair, J. McN. and Coulthard, R. M. (1975) *Towards an Analysis of Discourse*, London: Oxford University Press.

Smith, R. and Tomlinson, P. (1984) 'RAP: radio-assisted practice. Preliminary investigations of a new technique in teacher education', *Journal of Education for Teaching* 10: 119–34.

Sommer, R. (1969) *Personal Space*, Englewood Cliffs, N.J.: Prentice-Hall.

Stanworth, M. (1983) *Gender and Schooling*, London: Hutchinson.

Streeck, J. (1983) *Social Order in Child Communication: a Study in Microethnography, Pragmatics and Beyond* IV:8, Amsterdam: John Benjamin.

Torode, B. (1976) 'Teachers' talk and classroom discipline', in M. Stubbs and S. Delamont (eds) *Explorations in Classroom Observation*, London: Wiley.

Turner, G. (1983) *The Social World of the Comprehensive School*, London: Croom Helm.

Wheldall, K. and Glynn, T. (1989) *Effective Classroom Learning*, Oxford: Blackwell.

Woods, P. (1975) ' "Showing them up" in secondary school', in G. Chanan and S. Delamont (eds) *Frontiers of Classroom Research*, Slough: NFER.

Wragg, E. C. and Wood, E. K. (1984) 'Teachers' first encounters with their classes', in E. C. Wragg (ed.) *Classroom Teaching Skills*, London: Croom Helm.

Further reading

Neill, S. R. St J. (1991) *Classroom Nonverbal Communication*, London: Routledge.

Gives a more wide-ranging but academically oriented coverage than this book, and includes references to our research papers and the other evidence on which many statements made here are based.

Robertson, J. (1981) *Effective Classroom Control*, London: Hodder & Stoughton.
Calderhead, J. (1984) *Teachers' Classroom Decision-Making*, London: Holt, Rinehart & Winston.

Both these books survey a wider area than ours and relate classroom interaction to the broader issues of teaching in a way which we have not tried to emulate; Robertson, especially, takes a similar viewpoint and is particularly strong on analysing and dealing with unwanted behaviour. Calderhead's strength is curriculum decision-making, the school context in which the teacher works and the constraints under which she operates.

There are numerous guides to classroom control, for example:
McManus, M. (1989) *Troublesome Behaviour in the Classroom*, London: Routledge.

Rogers, B. (1991) *You Know the Fair Rule*, Harlow: Longman.
(Based on Australian work, and stresses the value and application of rules in maintaining discipline.)

Books on general non-verbal behaviour

Most of these books have little material directly related to education, but as we have emphasised in the text, most of the signals used in the classroom also occur widely in other contexts.

Bull, P. (1983) *Body Movement and Interpersonal Communication*, Chichester: Wiley.

An up-to-date and well-written general account of non-verbal communication, from a psychological viewpoint. There is a short section on non-verbal communication in education, in which Bull concludes that its importance is limited; but this conclusion is based on a limited number of studies in rather artificial situations.

Feldman, R. S. (ed.) (1982) *Development of Non-verbal Behavior in Children*, New York: Springer-Verlag.

A more technical book than Bull; a collection of articles, largely based on psychological experiments, covering the development of children's abilities to use and decode non-verbal behaviour. A valuable source-book, but only if you want technical detail.

Popular books on general non-verbal behaviour

Marsh, P. (ed.) (1988) *Eye to Eye*, London: Guild.
Morris, D. (1977) *Manwatching*, London: Triad Panther.

Two profusely illustrated popular books which give a general account of interpersonal skills; Morris puts more emphasis on the individual types of signal and their evolutionary background, while Marsh and his fellow-contributors emphasise different types of relationship and how they are expressed by the signals used.

Nierenberg, G. I. and Calero, H. H. (1983) *How to Read a Person like a Book*, Wellingborough: Thorsons.
Pease, A. (1981) *Body Language*, London: Sheldon.

These titles give a fair impression of these books which are well illustrated, but provocative rather than authoritative.

Sociological books covering classroom interaction

Beynon, J. (1985) *Initial Encounters in the Secondary School*, London: Falmer.

A readable account of how teacher–class relationships were established in a tough Welsh secondary school, which has been frequently referred to in the text.

Macpherson, J. (1983) *The Feral Classroom*, London: Routledge & Kegan Paul.
Turner, G. (1983) *The Social World of the Comprehensive School*, London: Croom Helm.

Two ethnographic books which show the influence of peer-group pressures on children's behaviour and school performance. As the titles imply, Turner's children were milder than MacPherson's. Turner has an interesting section on the ways in which children can conceal their challenges to the teacher, MacPherson one on 'seatmanship' – the manipulation of classroom seating position as a method of dealing with the teacher.

Author Index

Adams, R.S. 28
Armstrong, S. 100
Atkinson, M. 3
Baldwin, D. 161
Ball, S.J. 43
Beattie, G. 78, 108, 156
Bennett, N. 30
Beynon, J. 43–4, 46, 103, 130, 166, 169
Biddle, B.J. 28
Bossert, S.T. 30
Brazil, D. 12, 107
Brown, G.A. 100
Bull, P. 168, 185
Calderhead, J. 184
Caswell, C. 32. 44. 45
Cherlin, D.L. 29
Cockburn, A. 30
Coulthard, R. M. 12, 78, 107
Delamont, S. 25, 46
Denscombe, M. 45, 46, 155, 165
Desforges, C. 30
Docking, J.W. 2
Edmondson, R. 100
Ellis, A. 78, 156
Evans, K. 165
Furlong, V.J. 44, 110
Galton, M. 45
Gannaway, H. 185
Glynn, T. 29, 30
Goffman, E. 25, 164
Guy, J.J. 157

Hall, E.T. 26, 160
Harre, R. 31
Hayman, J. L. 104
Humphries, S. 133
Johns, C. 12, 107
Klinzing, H.G. 182–3, 185
Kounin, J.S. 68, 102, 130, 138, 157
Lawes, J.S. 183–4
Lister, C. 161
Macpherson, J. 29, 44, 56, 110
Marland, M. 29, 44, 161
Marsh, P. 31, 168
McNeill, D. 111–3
Moore, D.W. 29
Morris, D. 79, 84
Moskowitz, G. 104
Nash, R. 2
Neill, S.R.St.J. xiii, 100, 128, 133, 163–4, 182
Partington, J. 90, 132
Pollard, A. 56
Robertson, J. 8, 85
Rogers, B. 135
Rosser, E. 31
Rowe, M.B. 108, 118
Scheflen, A. 165–6
Scheflen, A.E. 165–6
Schwebel, A.E. 29
Sinclair, J.McN. 78, 107
Smith, R. 184
Sommer, R. 30

Stanworth, M. 156
Streeck, J. 31
Tisher, R.I. 182
Tomlinson, P. 184
Torode, B. 135
Turner, G. 42, 43, 46, 56, 103

Wheldall, K. 30
Wilkinson, B. 30
Willcocks, J. 45
Wood, E.K. 44, 65, 143
Woods, P. 141
Wragg, E.C. 44, 65, 143

Subject Index

ability, differences related to 56
abnormal behaviour 16 *see also* special needs
action zone 28
active learning 45, 64, 66, 187
age differences 14, 26, 30, 111, 128, 161–4,
    165, 178, 183–4, 185
air chop 136, Figs 7.11, 8.10; punch Fig 7.11;
    purse 112, 125, 135, Fig 7.17
alertness 63–4
anger, signals of 10, 12, 17, 22, 74, 96–7, 188,
    189, 192, Figs 2.1, 5.11, 8.1 *see also* threat
animal behaviour 17, 22
arms akimbo 81, 83
arms-fold 13, 53, 83, 84, 96, 157, Figs 2.9,
    4.6, 6.5, 6.14, 8.6, 8.7
assault 39–40, 42, 57, 61–2, 68, 130, 132–3,
    152, 154, 163, Figs 3.5, 5.7, 8.4, 8.5
assembly 92
assertiveness *see* dominant signals
attention 45, 64, 77–9, 85–9, 90, 92, 95, 97,
    102, 103, 107, 188, 190; distribution of 28,
    55, 103–4; signals 3, 11, 23, 63–4, 100–1,
    103, 108, 156–7, Figs 2.9, 6.15, 7.1–3
attitude to teaching 3
authority *see* dominant signals
autistic children 16

barrier signals 81, 83–5, 96, 102, 115, 117,
    131, 138, 157, Figs 6.5, 6.7, 6.8, 6.13, 6.13,
    8.8, 8.9, 8.13, 9.1

baton signals 102, 130, Figs 6.12, 8.8
beats *see* gestures
beckon 151, Fig 8.19
bite lip 85, Fig 6.11
boredom 3, 65, 125, Figs 5.5, 7.21, 7.22
bowed head 11; *see also* chin down
brow raise 112, 137, Figs 7.13, 8.11, 8.13, 9.2

'case law' 66, 68, 153
chair tipping 45, 64, 73, 99, 125, 149, 179,
    Figs 7.21, 9.16
challenges 22, 32, 39–41, 43, 45, 55, 144, 169,
    188, 189, 190, 191; closed 45, 52, 56–1, 62–
    5, 66–8, 70, 74, 125–6, 146, 151, 152, 158,
    Figs 4.1, 4.2, 4.4, 7.20–22, 8.15; open 52,
    53, 56–62, 68, 70, 74–6, 87–8, 125, 126,
    144, 149, 153, 166, Figs 4.3, 5.7–5.11, 7.23
child abuse 161, 178
chin up 11, 14, 22, 83, 97, Figs 2.5, 6.3, 8.6;
    down 11, 14, 22, 53, 83, Figs 2.6, 4.6, 6.4
classroom layout 25–6; social system 43, 46
closed challenges *see* challenges
clothing signals 13; pupils 21, 22, 23, 29, 31–
    2, 39, 62, 74, Figs 2.3, 2.6, 2.8, 3.2, 3.4, 5.9;
    teachers 31, 80, 83, 160
comprehension, signals of *see* understanding
    signals concentration frown 12, 96, 112,
    Figs 2.9, 6.15, 7.14
confidence, signals of 14, 77–8 *see also*
    dominant signals

conflict between pupils 8, Figs 1.3, 2.8, 3.5,
5.7, 5.11
control 1–2, 77–8, 109–10, 128–50, 166;
checks 57, 58, 60–2 *see also* flick checks;
signals *see* dominant signals
count off points Figs 7.12, 8.11, 8.12
courtship behaviour *see* flirting
coy expression 169, Fig 4.1
cultural variability 13–5, 111

decisiveness 87–9, 100, 102, 129, 130, 134,
138, 144
decoding 183–4
desk sit 41, 54, 80–1, 125, 160, 171, 179, Figs
8.2, 9.13–15
development of nonverbal skill 17, 111, 115,
183–4
deviant behaviour 42–3, 45, 48, 56, 191
disruptive behaviour xiv, 15, 44, 48, 51, 56,
57, 103, 104, 158, 166
dominant signals 10, 11–2, 13, 16, 22, 23–4,
39, 41, 81, 102, 110, 130–1, 146, 151–2,
158–60, 163–7, 169, 178, 179, 185, 188,
189, 192, Figs 2.3, 6.12, 7.3, 8.14, 8.18,
8.19, 9.9
dress *see* clothing signals

echo, behavioural 168, 179, Figs 9.8, 9.14
effective teachers 43–4, 55, 86–7, 100–2, 104,
105–8, 130, 135–41, 146, 164, 176–7 *see also*
experienced teachers
encouragement *see* enthusiasm, praise
enthusiasm xiv, 100–2, 120, 188, 190, 192
ethnic differences 13–5, 31, 96, 125
expectations 2
experienced teachers 43–4, 143, 153, 180–1,
184 *see also* effective teachers
explanations 99–100, 102, 103
eye contact *see* gaze
eyebrow flash 110 *see also* brow raise
eyes side Fig 9.2

facial expression 9–10, 11–2, 14, 96–7, 101,
112–3, 120, 123, 126, 154; neutral 64, 96,
102, Figs 6.15, 8.17; *see also* individual types
of expression
fairness 51, 70, 169, 180
feedback to speakers 78–9, 96 *see also* listening
signals
fending off gesture 102, 110, 130, Figs 2.8,
7.3
fidgeting 64, 102, 179
first lessons *see* initial encounters

flick check 52, 60–2, 97, Figs 4.3, 5.1
flirting 165–9, 178–9, Figs 9.5–8, 9.12
fold arms *see* arms fold
formal classrooms 4, 29, 110
forward baton 137, 149, Fig 6.12
forward lean 81, 108, 151, 137, 149, 179, Figs
7.2, 7.5, 8.1, 8.6, 8.16, 9.14
friends 2, 8, 163
frown 11–2, 95, 151, 185, Figs 4.6, 5.2, 79,
7.4, 7.13, 7.14, 8.1, 8.4, 8.5, 8.18, 8.19
fumbling 13, 40, 64, 73, 80, 85, 99, 102, 131,
149, 158, Figs 3.5, 5.4, 6.5, 6.6
furniture arrangement 25, 26, 30
frustration, signals of 64

gaze 9–10, 11, 14, 22, 23–4, 28, 30, 39, 41,
45, 52, 53–4, 57, 58, 59–60, 63, 64, 65, 66,
67, 68, 73, 75, 78–9, 95, 96–7, 101, 106,
107, 108, 125–6, 135–37, 151, 156, 158,
167–8, 178–9, 182, Figs 2.5, 2.7, 2.8, 2.9,
4.2, 5.8, 6.15, 7.2, 7.3, 7.5, 7.20, 7.22, 7.23,
8.2, 8.3, 8.6, 8.9, 8.10, 8.11, 8.12, 8.15, 9.2,
9.7, 9.8; aversion 11, 14, 22, 53, 65, 73, 75,
79, 115, 118, 123, 166, 169, Figs 2.6, 4.6,
6.1, 8.149.5, 9.6
gender differences *see* sex differences
gestures 10, 12–3, 14, 58, 63, 85, 111–7, 120,
123, 126, 130, 168, 182, 192; beats 13, 111,
113; emblematic 111; iconix 13, 111–2, Figs
7.7, 7.11; metaphorix 13, 107, 111–3, 125,
156, Figs 7.5, 7.9, 7.10, 7.12, 7.17–7.19
grooming 13, 64, 80, 85, 86, 115 Figs 6.6, 6.7
group work 66

hand forward Fig 7.3; to face 85, 115, Fig 6.8;
to mouth 169, Figs 4.1, 6.8
hands in pockets 23, 80, 102, 130, 151, 157,
Fig 8.17; on hips 13, 81, 83, 151, 157, Figs
4.5, 5.2, 6.2, 8.2, 8.3, 8.18, 9.1, 9.7
harassing peers 23, 39–40, 54, 68, 176, Figs
2.8, 3.5, 5.7, 5.11
head cant 11, 63, 96, 101, 110, 178, Figs 6.15,
7.2, 7.6, 9.10; position 11, 101, 107, 185,
Fig 7.1 *see also* chin up, chin down; prop 64,
125–6, Figs 5.5, 5.10, 7.21–23
help from other teachers 8, 118, 133–5, 149,
150, 152, 153
hesitancy *see* uncertainty signals
hiding 59, Fig 5.10
high achieving pupils 46
humour 97, 136–7, 138, 143–4, 152, 154, 169

iconic gestures *see* gestures

ideographic gestures *see* gestures
illustrative gestures *see* gestures
individual differences 15–6; distance 9–11, 14, 15, 24, 26–8, 41, 53, 75, 152, 156, 159–61, 167–9, 185, Figs 3.1, 4.5, 8.14, 9.3, 9.4, 9.10
ineffective teachers 102–3, 104–5, 115, 131–2, 157–8
informal classrooms 4, 11, 26, 45, 110, 165
informal social behaviour 2–3, 23, 26, 30–1, 34, 78–9, 96, 108, 109–10, 111, 112–3, 115, 128, 144, 155, 156–7, 161, 171, 178, 179, Figs 3.3, 3.4, 4.1–4, 9.13
initial encounters 6–8, 44, 65–6, 103–7, 144, 149–50, 152–3
intention movements 11, 80–1, 138
interaction set 23, 44, 66, 68, 74–5, Figs 2.8, 5.2, 5.10, 5.11
interest 12, 103, 155–7, 188, 189
interpersonal distance see individual distance
intonation 9–10, 12, 41, 53, 63, 96, 101, 102, 107–8, 118, 135–37, 138, 159–60, 182, 185; animated 12, 101, 107, 108, 130; emphatic 12, 54, 97, 105; proclaiming 12; referring 12
involvement in work 45, 57, 58, 66–7, Figs 5.6, 5.7, 5.9

joining hands 96, Figs 2.9, 6.13

kneeling 11, 160, Fig 9.4

leaders (pupils) 31, 41, 44
leaning 11; pupils 45, 64, 73, 75, 125–6, 168, Figs 2.8, 7.21, 8.3; teacher 80, 81, 123, 125, 158, 160, 179, Figs 6.1, 6.2, 7.16, 9.17
legal requirements 90
lesson segments 77
lip licking 85, Fig 6.9; press 85, Figs 6.9, 6.10
listening signals 101–2, 105, 156–7, 168

marker signals 78, 113–5
metaphoric gestures *see* gestures
minus face *see* chin down
mouth hiding *see* hand to mouth
movement around classroom 26, 29, 39, 40–1, 45, 53, 63, 64–5, 75, 80–1, 105, 135–6, 149, 151, 157–8; around school 25
moving pupils' position 23–4, 28–30, 34, 38, 40, 44, 75–6, 138, 163, Fig 9.9

nod 96, 108, 156, 168, 169
noise 45–6, 53, 57, 66, 95, 97, 123, 149
nonverbal leakage 81

open sesame gesture Fig 7.10
overlappingness 157

palm back 125, Fig 7.19; down 110, Fig 7.3; forward 13, Fig 7.3; side 125, Fig 7.18; up Fig 7.9
pantomiming 13, 111, 143, Fig 7.8
pauses in speech 96, 118, 137
personal and social education 123–4, 176–7
personal space *see* individual distance
plus face *see* chin up
pointing 13, 53, 66, 97, 110, 111, Figs 2.7, 5.2, 5.8, 5.11, 7.7, 9.3 9.4 *see also* baton signals
position in classroom; pupils *see* seating position; teacher 29, 64–5
postural echo *see* echo, behavioural
posture 9–11, 14, 21, 23, 31, 45, 52, 57, 58–9, 64, 74, 78, 118, 120, 135, 149, 154, 156, 157, 168, 179, 192, Figs 4.3, 5.10 *see* individual postures for other illustrations
practical lessons 45, 66, 90, 95, 103, 104–5, 178
praise xiv, 105–6, 163, 176–7, Fig 9.11
primary school children 165, 183–4 *see also* age differences
property, children's 34, 76, 152–4
public speaking 3–4
punishment 8
pushing 45, Figs 2.8, 3.5, 5.7
puzzle frown 12, 23, 106, 112, Figs 2.9, 7.15

questions 104, 105–7, 111, 118, 176–7, 180–1

racial differences *see* ethnic differences
registration 89
relative height 11, 25, 81, 130, 159–60, Figs 9.32, 9.4, 9.7, 9.11, 9.13–16
relative importance of nonverbal signals xvi, 184–6
relaxation 22, 39, 40, 41, 52, 64, 79–80, 102, 124, 125, 130, 137, 151, 171, 179, Figs 4.2, 8.17, 9.13, 9.16, 9.17
room arrangement *see* furniture arrangement
row seating 30
rules 22, 23, 41, 42–3, 74, 89–90, 133–41, 149, 153, Fig 2.8

sad brow 102, 125, 132, Figs 7.16, 8.14
sarcasm 106, Fig 7.4
sanctions, disciplinary 3, 4
seating position 11, 16, 25–31, 34, 38, 41, 44, 68, 176

self-awareness 156, 183–4, 189
self-esteem 103, 105–7, 155–6
self-holding 84, 96, Figs 2.9, 6.5, 6.13, 6.14, 8.8, 8.9, 8.13
self-pointing 106, 115, Fig 8.9
sex differences xi, 15, 16, 156, 163–9, 171, 178–9
shouting 10, 45, 66, 74, 95, 97, 130, 149–50, Figs 5.8, 5.11, 8.1
showing up 63, 141–4
silence (in speech) 108, 112, 118, *see also* wait time
skill *see* development of nonverbal skill
smile 12, 13, 14, 16, 41, 58, 65, 74–5, 96, 101, 105, 106, 108, 126, 130–1, 136–7, 149, 151, 152, 163, 168, 169, Figs 4.4, 4.5, 5.10, 7.1, 7.2, 7.4, 7.5, 8.3, 8.6, 8.12, 8.13, 8.16, 9.2, 9.5–8, 9.10, 9.12, 9.13
social behaviour, informal *see* informal social behaviour
space 9–11, 25–8
special needs 6, 8, 15–6, 176–7, 180–1, 187, Fig. 1.2
status signals 25 *see also* dominant signals
stress 13, 53, 83–7, 137–8, 179
student teachers 143–4, 183–4, 185
students (college / university) 29, 157
subordinate signals 11, 14, 17, 22, 53, 75–6, 83, 131–2, Figs 2.6, 4.6
subjects 5, 118
surprise, signals of 12, 13, 105

table seating 30
talking by pupils 22, 39, 58, 66–8, 123, 146,
149, 151, 179, Figs 2.7, 3.3, 3.4, 4.2, 4.3, 4.4, 5.1, 5.8, 5.10, 5.11, 8.4, 8.15, 9.13
see also noise
threat 22, 23, 53, 97, 126, 129–30, 151, 152, Figs 2.2, 2.5, 2.8, 8.1, 8.18
throwing 74, 97, Figs 5.3, 5.9
timing of signals 78
tone of voice *see* intonation
touch 10, 14, 15, 16, 21, 52–3, 84, 138, 161–5, 169, 171, 176–7, 178–9, 180–1, Figs 4.5, 8.14, 9.5, 9.6, 9.9–12 *see also* flirting
training xiii–vi, 2, 182–4, 186–94
transitions between activities 13, 77, 78, 138
turning round (by pupils) 39, 52, 68, 75, Figs 3.3, 3.4, 4.4, 5.11

uncertainty signals 15, 40, 79, 83–6, 96, 97, 102–3, 117–8, 125, 138, 157–8, 179, Figs 6.4–11, 6.13, 6.14, 7.16, 9.1, 9.15 *see also* subordinate signals
understanding, signals of 183
upward baton Figs 6.12, 8.8

vacuum hold 108, 125, Figs 7.5, 7.10, 7.19
video xiii, 183, 189–90, 191, 193–4

wait time 10, 108
wide eyes Fig 9.2
wielding 10
withitness 68, 130, 156, 160
work involvement *see* involvement in work

yawning 65, Fig 5.5